A MEMOIR OF EXPERIENCE,
STRENGTH, AND HOPE

# *Cancer*
# TAUGHT
# ME

## ANGELA ROLOSON

For Tim, Rae, Hunter, and Abbey.
You have been and continue to be my reason.

# Contents

# Preface

According to the American Cancer Association, one in eight women in the United States will be diagnosed with breast cancer during their lifetime. Cancer has touched the life of nearly everyone I talk to. Either we have fought the battle ourselves, we have helped someone else to navigate it, or we know someone who has made this journey.

I could recount for you the nights I cried after my kids were in bed. I could share how scared we all were and how hard we all pretended not to be. I could tell you how much chemotherapy sucks. All of that would make this just another cancer memoir, and I didn't want to write just another sad book about cancer.

My goal was to write a different kind of cancer memoir. I wanted to share the challenges I encountered on my journey in the hope that it might provide some sort of common ground for those of you who are currently struggling, have struggled, or know and love others who have struggled, especially those who have also battled addiction. More importantly, I wanted to share the lessons I learned through this journey. With years of hindsight, I can see how much I changed and grew during that time in my life and through those struggles.

If I hadn't been diagnosed with cancer, maybe I would have been stuck in those same bad habits and negative mindsets. To that end, I've tried as honestly as possible to share the truth of my life during that time as well as the hard-fought lessons. It was my intention that no matter what your experience has been, you will find something here that may be useful to you in some season of your life. If you have just been diagnosed with cancer, I hope you find compassion, understanding, and hope; if you have a loved one battling cancer, I want to encourage you because the job of caretaker is difficult; and for those not yet touched by cancer, I hope there are lessons in these pages that can be applied to other hardships.

Whatever seemingly insurmountable obstacles you have faced or are facing, ultimately my hope is that in these pages you will find something that is helpful navigating that journey. The things I learned from cancer, after all, have a little to do with cancer and everything to do with life. They have shaped who I am today, and they illustrate the triumph of the human spirit. My cancer was stage 1 and my cancer journey from start to finish was less than a year. I was lucky. Everyone's journey is unique, and I am certainly no expert. All I can offer is my "experience, strength, and hope." That is what I have endeavored to do in this book.

# Chapter 1

---

# Being Cancer-Free Doesn't Fix Everything

"Difficult roads can lead to beautiful destinations."
Kia Wynn, Oral Cancer Survivor

I had reached the end of chemotherapy and I had one more scheduled appointment with my oncologist, Dr. Adebayo. Most of my appointments had been with his physician's assistant and leading to this follow-up, I wished I was seeing Ellen again. Her genuine, sincere conversational style would have made this day so much easier. Since this all began eight months earlier, I had not attended a single appointment, including surgeries and chemotherapy, by myself. This day would be different.

Cade had attended every one of my appointments. Early on, he took notes so that I wouldn't miss or forget any information I might need in order to make a decision. Later, he brought a sense of lightness when things seemed too burdensome, and sometimes he would simply extend his hand and gently massage my back when he noticed me becoming overwhelmed. Now that I was cancer-free, he had bailed. He had never intended to stay, I thought. It was just a bad look to break up with someone when they've just told you they have cancer. Now, years later, I know that isn't fair. I do not know what he was thinking, but I do know he didn't have to stay and take care of me. I did not see it that way in Dr. Adebayo's office, though.

It had been two weeks since Cade and I parted ways and I hadn't yet figured out how to navigate the rest of this journey, as well as the rest of my life, without him by my side. I had relied more on him throughout all of this than I had ever relied on another human being. He exhibited strength when I was unable to, and it was going to require more work than I wanted to put forth to find the inner strength that everyone else believed I had.

As I sat in the examining room, listening to the humming of the fan, my brain spun with thoughts of how alone I felt. I wanted to hold it together for the appointment. I had portrayed strength numerous times during this journey when I didn't truly feel that way. If I faked my way through this appointment, then I could go home and indulge in self-pity again.

That poor doctor came in expecting to see me doing cartwheels. Instead, he found me crying and the more he tried to help, the harder I cried. I was inconsolable. He attempted again and again to put life into perspective for me.

"You beat cancer. Nothing can be as bad as that."

"Based on the information available to us, Angela, you are free of cancer."

"We all hit rough patches in life."

I was aware of these things. They were all logical, but I was not. And his cheerful demeanor was making me feel worse, not better. Trust me when I say the last thing I wanted to do was to break down in his office, but I cried for almost ten minutes. I lacked any explanation for what I was experiencing, at least one that would make sense to him or even to me, but I knew I had to try.

"I guess I've struggled a little with depression through the cancer treatments. I just thought I'd feel better after the treatments were done and, if anything, I feel worse."

"Angela, you are cancer-free. You should be celebrating."

There was nothing I could say in response. I was confident he was right, but celebrating was the last thing on my mind. I had always had issues with body image and during the last eight months I had been struggling with an increase in those issues. Add to that the end of a relationship I had hoped would last forever, and I found myself in a bad place. I felt piled on. Despite the fact that I was cancer-free and should have been filled with happiness, the thought of celebrating alone brought on more waves of sadness.

Dr. A was concerned about me and could not emphasize that enough. When I reassured him that I had no suicidal thoughts and I certainly hadn't devised a strategy for executing such a hypothetical scenario, he prescribed an antidepressant and advised me to arrange a therapy session.

"I'd like to see you in four months, instead of six, Angela. Hopefully you will be doing better then." I finally saw something other than that over-the-top smile on his face, and I didn't like it. His furrowed brow and downturned mouth left me feeling like a burden. There is nothing worse than being on the receiving end of that look of pity when you want to be strong and resilient.

I left his office discouraged with myself. I had wanted to be done with all of this cancer crap. In two weeks, I was having my implants put in and that was supposed to be the symbolic end of this for me. For eight months, all I had thought about was winning this battle. I had longed to hear the words "you are cancer-free." While I was fighting cancer, it made sense that I would burst into tears at a moment's notice, but I saw today as reaching the summit of the mountain after a demanding climb. I envisioned some type of elation, or at least relief, that I had made it. I hated that this break-up had the ability to take that away from me. I never wanted to be the girl who defined herself by whether she was in a relationship, or by what a boy thought about her, but that's who I had become.

My self-esteem was the lowest it had been since I quit drinking. That low self-esteem fed my depression. It told me that if Cade didn't want me, no one would want me. It said that he left the relationship because I had cancer and was no longer attractive. It shouted that cancer had taken from me everything that made me worthy of love. None of that was true, but depression doesn't tell the truth.

I thought being cancer-free would fix everything, but it couldn't fix this. As I left Dr. Adebayo's office, I thought that I wanted my relationship back. That wasn't it. My relationship with Cade had been far from perfect. The real issue was that I didn't know who I was anymore. I used to be part of a couple; I shared friends and experiences with my partner. Who was I as a single person in recovery? The loss of this relationship left me floundering, but that wasn't all. I used to be the girl with boobs; then I was the girl with cancer. Now who was I? I felt lost and being cancer-free couldn't fix that. Cancer had changed everything and I would need to figure out how to navigate life now that cancer didn't define every minute of it. I no longer had cancer, but that didn't mean everything in my life was fixed.

# Chapter 2

# Sometimes Food Is the Only Answer

"Let food be thy medicine and medicine be thy food."
Hippocrates

C ancer arrived as an unwelcome visitor, sitting on my front porch, demanding my attention. I was not happy to find it waiting there, but I continued to play the unwilling host until a plan was in place to show my cancer to the door. This was quite the process, as you might imagine, but in the end it has been worth the struggle. Cancer left my place in a bit of a mess, and I'm conscious that it has kept the key in case it decides to visit again. I continue to be hopeful, though, that all I will be left with is the memory of time spent with a stranger I never expected to meet.

My journey began on September 21, 2011, with a routine screening mammogram. Despite being just forty-six, I underwent yearly mammograms starting at age thirty-five due to my family history. I had to advocate for this schedule because all the breast cancer cases occurred on the paternal side of my family and previous research indicated that it was not a risk factor for me. My grandmother had breast cancer prior to age fifty, though, and it later metastasized, leading to her passing in 1983. Despite being diagnosed with breast cancer twice, my aunt, my father's oldest sister, has survived and is now over eighty years old. I mention this to assure you that I had previously experienced the smashing of "the girls" in the cold metal mammogram machine. It was one of those things I did because I was a rule follower. The doctor would say, "Time for your annual mammogram," so I'd schedule the mammogram. A couple days later, I would check my online health portal and it would report "normal" and I would go on with life until the next annual smashing of the girls.

Sometimes, following the mammogram, I would need an ultrasound to rule out any need for concern, but so far the ultrasound had always ruled out cancer. The doctor on those occasions would usually mention that my breast tissue was dense, which sometimes caused issues with detecting things on the mammogram. I accepted this explanation without question. Following my mammogram in 2011, my online portal told the story before I received the phone call. Three concerning spots were identified, prompting the next step—an ultrasound. Having gone through an ultrasound previously, I was sure the radiologist would detect what the mammogram couldn't due to my dense breast tissue and everything would be fine. Ten years later, I would read about the heightened cancer risk linked to dense breast tissue, but on that day in the fall of 2011, I didn't have any worries.

It didn't take long after the ultrasound for the radiologist to tell me the ultrasound did not show a conclusive result, and we scheduled a biopsy for October 17. While I hadn't been concerned about the ultrasound, the same couldn't be said for the biopsy. I found the word "biopsy" to be triggering. I guess I had watched a few too many cancer movies. My heart raced as I heard those words. I tried to believe my worries were unfounded, yet I could not rid myself of the apprehension. It didn't help that I had to wait for almost three weeks to have the biopsy done.

When I arrived at the clinic the day of the biopsy, after putting on the thin hospital gown and attempting to tie it to hide all the pertinent parts of my anatomy, the technician told me to lie on the table. The first thing they did after I got settled was untie my gown to access my right breast. So much for any modesty.

Obtaining samples from the three small spots seemed to take forever. The clinic allocated one hour for my appointment, but time dragged on as I lay with my breast exposed on the hard, narrow table in the cold, stark white room. If I made the slightest movement to either side, I was certain I would end up on the floor. My back spasmed as I tried to lay as still as possible, hoping that would make things go more quickly. The longer I lay on the table, the more uncomfortable I grew. Could the temperature in this room have dropped ten degrees from when we first began? I shivered as I tried to focus on what the radiologist was saying: "These spots are deep, so it's taking a little longer to get the samples." I remained silent, unsure how I was supposed to respond.

As I lay there, trying to control my thoughts, I remembered being scheduled for an ultrasound exam following an irregular mammogram several years before. On that day, I sat in the waiting room for over two hours. The receptionist kept offering to reschedule for another day, but I was nervous and I didn't want to wait. She told me they were doing a biopsy, and it was taking longer than expected. I recall saying, "It's okay. Obviously, that woman needs the time more than I do today." In the end, I did agree to reschedule. Now, years later, I was the one who needed the time. That did not make me feel better, but it did make me wonder how things had ended for that woman. I shivered once again, but this time it wasn't because of the cold.

"Remember," the radiologist said, bringing me back to the present and my exposed breast, "pressure is okay but pain is not, so if you're experiencing any pain, let me know and we can give you more Lidocaine." I couldn't see the clock, but I was sure it had been longer than an hour based on how many doses of Lidocaine they had already administered.

To take my mind off things, I watched the process unfolding on the screen next to me. After removing a small tissue sample, the radiologist inserted a tiny metal marker to identify the biopsied areas. That way, future radiologists could identify the areas that had already been biopsied. I realized as I watched the screen that it was possible to block out my negative thoughts by pretending I was watching someone else's procedure. I now call this my first out-of-body experience. The biopsy proved to be fascinating from the perspective of an outsider.

At long last, the radiologist said, "Okay, that should do it. We just need one more quick mammogram to make sure we can see the markers." As she made her way to the other room to prepare for that, I asked Cade how long we had been here. "A little over four hours, hon," he said as he glanced at his watch before standing up to stretch his back. Four hours. The procedure, which should have taken a quarter of the time, ended up lasting for four hours. How could that end with a positive result? I groaned as I sat up, pausing to let the spasm in my back pass.

Many times during the next year, I would view this four-hour biopsy as my first sign that time would not move forward as quickly as I would have liked. This journey would be filled with appointments I dreaded, decisions I wished I didn't have to make, and waiting anxiously for answers. And it all started on an otherwise beautiful fall day during Breast Cancer Awareness month.

Alone, I battled my anxiety for hours that night. Maybe it was selfish, but I was not willing to share my fears with anyone. Not with Cade; not with my family; not with my friends. If I said it out loud, it might make it true. I needed to pretend everything was normal and maybe, just maybe, things would end positively. Finally, I convinced myself I would receive positive news from the clinic in a couple days and I fell asleep in the early morning hours.

The next day, as I pulled into the Festival Foods parking lot with my fifteen-year-old daughter sitting in the passenger seat, I received a call from the clinic. My heart raced as I answered the phone. The radiologist spoke clearly and concisely. "Angela, we have your biopsy results. All three spots are cancer." A current ran through my body as I struggled to remain calm. There it was.

That was the answer. It wasn't what I wanted to hear, but it was an answer.

Friends have expressed disbelief at the manner in which I received this news, but I am thankful. If the radiologist had invited me to the clinic for a discussion about my results, I would have realized it was bad news anyway, and if she had given a long explanation, I would have broken down right there in the parking lot of the grocery store.

I didn't cry; I couldn't. I had to be a mom. I used my teacher training to "be professional" and scheduled an appointment the next day for a surgical consult. My daughter and I have discussed this moment since. She tells me she was sure something was wrong, but she wanted to believe me when I told her it was nothing. And in that moment, I needed to believe that she believed me. So I hung up the phone, turned to her, and asked, "Do you want tacos or pizza for supper?"

# Chapter 3

## Pause, Pray, Proceed

"The quieter you become, the more you can hear."
Buddha

When I received my diagnosis in 2011, I was working as a high school English teacher and, as luck would have it, a coworker in my department fought breast cancer the year before. The next day, when I talked to Karen, she told me to "stay off the internet." This is sound advice. On the internet, you may find factual, helpful information, but you will also find every worst-case scenario and more horror stories than you can take in your fragile emotional state. Did I pay attention to the words of this intelligent woman who understood what she was talking about? Of course not.

Fortunately, I managed to not descend too far into the black hole that is Google. I wish I had listened, though, and my best advice if you find yourself in a situation like this is to wait for the doctor. The clinic will provide you with all the necessary information, having already removed the misleading and terrifying content. Trust science, not the internet! Cancer aside, this is valuable advice. The second piece of advice she provided me with was to take a notetaker to the appointment with the surgeon. She said, "You are smart and capable, but they will go over so much and you will be overwhelmed." What an understatement.

On October 19, less than a month after my initial mammogram, I met with the surgeon, Dr. Lancaster, for the first time. I folded my hands tightly in my lap to control the shaking and I sat staring at them, lost in my thoughts. I knew I had cancer, but I did not know what would come next. The words "you have cancer" are terrifying. It was all I had been able to think about since I'd heard them, but I still couldn't wrap my brain around it. What did that even mean? I knew survivors, and I had attended funerals of friends and family members who did not survive. I had to be okay; I saw no other option. And part of that for me was maintaining this concrete wall that surrounded me, refusing to share my fears with anyone. My tough exterior had gotten me this far in life; no reason to abandon it now.

My eyes scanned the room hoping to find answers, but all that greeted me was a sterile white exam room minus the table. Even the doctors' offices in the clinic looked institutional. I looked up when the surgeon walked into the room. I am not sure what I expected, but this was not the picture in my head of Dr. Lancaster. Everyone I spoke to told me he was the best, so I suppose I was picturing this refined looking surgeon, maybe wearing a dress shirt and tie and neatly groomed. Instead, he sported a white lab coat, his hair was tousled, and his eyebrows bushy, giving the appearance of a unibrow.

The appointment lasted for an hour and when I left that day, the only thing I retained was that Dr. Lancaster believed a lumpectomy might eliminate all the cancer. However, to confirm this, he ordered a breast MRI to verify that there were no additional abnormalities that the mammogram had not detected. I'm not sure how much of my lack of focus stemmed from the trauma of the cancer diagnosis and how much was due to my distraction. I couldn't help it. As he talked, the unibrow moved, and I found my eyes repeatedly drawn to it. Fortunately, Cade took notes, and despite not being in a fit state of mind to review them that night, I would often refer to them later.

The MRI on October 27 marked the next step in my journey down the road of impossible decisions. I had experienced just one MRI before, so I knew the technician would place me inside a compact tube, having provided me with headphones to lessen the intense clanging noise of the machine capturing images. I am claustrophobic and let's just say I was not excited about this.

This MRI differed from my first one, though. They positioned me on my stomach, leaving an open area for my breasts. Laying at the bottom of the tube with the camera positioned above me I was able to observe the open space below, stretching all the way down to the floor. This experience proved to be significantly better than my previous MRI, at least until I attempted to stand up thirty minutes later. My forty-six-year-old back spasmed, taking my breath away. I hadn't stretched out on my stomach without moving for a long time and my back wasn't a fan, so getting up was a slow process. In the end, the MRI found no cancer in the left breast, but there was "an increased presence of potential cancer" in the right. I was aware that this reduced the chances of a lumpectomy completely eradicating my cancer. Anger bubbled just below the surface. Why couldn't I just get some good news for a change?!

Because there was still a possibility that I would need a mastectomy, I next met with the plastic surgeon, Dr. Garett, to discuss potential reconstruction options if we went that route. While Dr. Lancaster's appearance surprised me, Dr. Garett looked exactly like what I would expect in a plastic surgeon. He entered the room wearing not only a dress shirt and tie, but a suit coat as well. A stereotypical plastic surgeon, Dr. Garett was an attractive man. Cade described him as "pretty." I would have to agree. He was not ruggedly handsome, but he sure was nice to look at. I'm certain that his pleasant demeanor drew in business in the plastic surgery industry, but I wasn't prepared to talk about implants or reconstruction with him or anyone else. I liked my boobs the way they were—well, minus the cancer, of course. Being a realist, I acknowledged the possible necessity of a mastectomy, but I didn't like it. Dr. Garett did give me information I would later appreciate, but first I needed to somehow make this difficult decision.

There was one remaining test that might help me decide which surgery option to choose, but the difficulty proved to be getting my insurance company to agree to pay for it. What I was requesting was a genetic test to determine whether I had mutations in the BRCA1 and BRCA2 genes. If I did have this mutation, it would mean I had a higher risk of future breast and ovarian cancer. It would also mean that my children should have testing done to determine whether they also had an increased risk of cancer. The insurance company's response was that they had up to ninety days to determine whether this would be covered. In frustration, I said, "Ninety days?! I have cancer. I need this test to determine what surgery I should have." If you've ever had a dispute with a health insurance company, you are probably not surprised to hear that they simply read back to me the same script stating that within the next ninety days the decision would be forwarded to the clinic.

Fortunately, my workplace had an insurance advocate and so I contacted her. She assured me that because President Obama had signed the Women's Healthcare Act into law, the insurance company had to cover this testing, so on November 2, I had a blood draw for genetic testing. I decided if it came back positive, I would know that I was supposed to choose a mastectomy. The test came back negative. Nothing would make this easy for me, but at least my kids wouldn't have any higher chance of contracting breast cancer than they already did.

During this time, I was not in a good place emotionally. I remembered this feeling from my drinking days before I found my way to recovery from alcoholism. I didn't want to think anymore; I didn't want to feel anymore. I just wanted someone to tell me what I should do. I kept going to meetings, and I surrounded myself with my friends in recovery. At those meetings, I remembered the tools I used in the days when I first stopped drinking. I refocused on the phrase "one day at a time" and I remembered that early in sobriety, I sometimes needed to take life one breath at a time. It helped me get through the hard days, so that's what I did again in October 2011.

I was living in my own personal hell, but I didn't want to share the news of my cancer with my kids until I had a definite plan, so I met again with my surgeon. This time, I managed to maintain my focus, despite the distraction of the unibrow. In the past, I have seen specialists who spewed medical jargon and appeared so hurried that I simply agreed with whatever they recommended and later searched online for an explanation I could comprehend.

Dr. Lancaster was different. He explained things for me until I understood. It was unlike anything I had encountered before in a medical setting. Dr. L said he might be able to get all three spots with a lumpectomy, but he was more certain he could remove all the cancerous tissue with a mastectomy. I thought, Of course you can. You are just a giant ray of fucking sunshine! I listened as he explained the procedures, and Cade took notes. That left the remaining suspicious areas identified by the MRI, but without conducting a biopsy on each of them, there was no way to ascertain what we were dealing with. The more I traveled along this road, the more confused I became and the less certain I felt about whether I should have a lumpectomy or a mastectomy.

In this season of my life, I had not been inside a church for a long time. This was a bit of a sticky point in my recovery because relying on a higher power of some kind is a big part of my twelve-step program. Throughout my recovery, I had grappled with this. Sometimes I found spirituality in the feeling of riding on the back of a motorcycle in nature. I mean, when you look at the beauty of the scenery on a gorgeous fall day in Wisconsin, it's difficult not to believe there might be some higher power. I wasn't sure at this point that I had faith in anything, though, least of all myself. Still, my sponsor advised me to pray for guidance with the surgical decision. Over the previous two years, I learned to listen to my sponsor even when I disagreed with her advice, so I made it a daily habit to pray—just in case there existed some higher power that could offer divine guidance. I was willing to try anything.

A week later, as I sat in the surgeon's office, I had an epiphany. I needed objective data. I needed to remove emotion, allowing the logical part of my brain to assume control.

"How likely is recurrence after a lumpectomy?" I asked.

"Approximately 15-20 percent."

"And a mastectomy?"

"Less than 5 percent."

After an extended period of silence, I spoke. "My grandmother and aunt both had breast cancer on multiple occasions. Would that change the numbers?"

I'm sure that this request for his thoughts made the surgeon uncomfortable. His face clouded over. No conclusive answer existed, but he held a professional opinion rooted in his experience as a surgeon. After pausing, he sighed. "I would put it closer to 30-35 percent."

I heard myself saying, "I want to go with the bilateral mastectomy." The weird thing is that I do not know where these words came from. When I entered that office, I was nowhere close to making *this* decision. As I uttered the words, I wasn't aware that I had made a decision. There is no explanation I can provide for this other than divine intervention. This was the first time I remember anything like this happening, but in the years since, I have learned that when I keep an open mind in the moments when I stop overthinking things, no matter how brief those moments may be, I often receive the answer from God. In this moment, I knew my prayers had paid off and I could sense God's guidance. I still didn't like it, but I felt just a little less alone—at least in that moment.

# Chapter 4

---

# Life Is Not Predictable

"If life were predictable it would cease to be life, and be
without flavor."
Eleanor Roosevelt

P rior to my diagnosis, I had discovered some measure of peace
with the trajectory of my life: My two oldest children, now
young adults, lived on their own; I had been sober for over two
years, and was taking actions to become healthier; I had adjusted
to being a single parent and my two youngest children and I were
building a better life; I was co-parenting with my ex-husband; and
I was in a relationship that made me happy most of the time. I like
control. Lack of control caused much of the unhappiness in my
marriage. It's also why I felt miserable during my drinking days.
For the first time in my life, I believed I was in control.

Control is an illusion, though, and that's the truth. The only
thing we can truly control is our reaction to things. We cannot
control the universe. Shit happens! Right when my life was going
well, a radiologist dared to utter the "C word."

Cancer is one hell of a brick wall to hit going seventy miles per
hour. Perception is key, though, and I am now far enough removed
from my cancer diagnosis and all that came with it to see that
everybody is dealing with something. During my cancer journey I

was able to remind myself that there were plenty of people facing more challenging circumstances than I was. Did that prevent me from succumbing to thoughts of self-pity? No, and I had the right to those moments. I had cancer, for crying out loud. The thing that it did, though, was aid me in regaining my composure, shaking off any setbacks, and carrying on with life to the best of my ability. Every day during those six months, I repeated the same statement as I looked in the mirror: "There are plenty of people who have it worse than you." Some days I believed it more than others, and some days I wanted to scream, "I don't fucking care." In the end, reminding myself every day that I was not the only one struggling helped me keep things in perspective over time, and it kept me from sinking too far into isolation and depression. That doesn't mean it didn't suck and it doesn't mean I was easy to be around. In fact, there were days I didn't want to be around myself.

Once I settled on which surgery I would have, the next obstacle in front of me was the discussion with my kids. My oldest daughter, Rae, was already upset with me. At twenty, she knew I should have received answers from the clinic by now. I admitted she was right, but I begged her to not tell her younger siblings. Her brother was in a play at school, and I wanted him to experience this last bit of "normal" before I disrupted their lives.

Before long, though, the time for that conversation arrived. I enjoyed a pleasant dinner with Cade and my two youngest children, and then Cade excused himself to give me and the kids some alone time. I looked up at Hunter and Abbey and then, looking down at the table again, I said, "I need to talk to the two of you for a minute."

Hunter, seeing me uncharacteristically somber, asked, "What's going on, mom?"

As I studied both him and his sister, I said, "There's no easy way to tell you this." I then shared the doctors' findings and told them about my scheduled surgery. Then I asked if they had questions.

Abbey asked all the normal stuff. "Do you need to have chemo? Will your hair fall out? How will you work? Do Rae and Tim know?

Does Dad know?" I answered each of her questions to the best of my ability.

Then I looked at Hunter and said, "Do you have questions, Hunt?"

His gaze lingered on me. Then my always funny, always sarcastic son simply asked, with tears in his eyes, "Are you going to be alright?"

I replied, "That's the plan."

We sat, eyes locked, at a loss for words. We would have more conversations about my cancer, but this one was by far the hardest. It was more than sharing a diagnosis with my kids; this information would change their lives forever. They would never again be the same carefree kids they had been before that night. I had expected that having this conversation would provide me some emotional relief, but instead, I experienced a sense of sadness afterwards—sadness both for myself and for my children. Just like many previous nights, Cade held me as I cried until I drifted off to sleep.

Sometimes the road of life is smooth, but there are potholes along the road that slow down our progress. I had been making progress; the kids and I had been making progress together. In time, I would realize this obstacle on the road, albeit a significant one, didn't have to stop us. It took a lot of time to take the detour, one I didn't want to be on, but there was nothing I could do to alter that. Following the signs provided the solution. For me, those signs included listening to the advice of doctors, processing tough days with close friends, and attending recovery meetings that reminded me the world doesn't revolve around me.

This hadn't always been true.

Cancer taught me that life is not predictable, and it is not easy. No matter what our individual struggles are, we all have them. And, sadly, it is through those struggles that we grow the most. On this journey, I grew spiritually, and I learned so much about the world and the people in it. I wish I could have done that without it affecting my children, but that's just how things turned out. We did the best we could day by day and we all came out the other side, bruised and a little battered, but still standing.

# Chapter 5

# People Are Good--Even Teenagers

"I have this theory that if one person can go out of their way to show compassion, then it will start a chain reaction of the same. People will never know how far a little kindness can go." Rachel Joy Scott, Student, First Victim of the Columbine High School Massacre

Before every big test when I was a student, I told my friends I was going to fail. I had done the homework; I had studied. By anticipating the worst, however, I was convinced that I wouldn't be disappointed. I'm not sure exactly when this became my approach to life, but for as long as I could remember expectations felt like a mountain standing in front of me, its summit beckoning. In fourth grade, my first experience with letter grades, my math grade dipped briefly to a C. My mom made it clear to me, in no uncertain terms that a C was not an acceptable grade for me. I had always tested in the top 98th percentile in reading and math and I thrived on the positive response I garnered from teachers.

The more I achieved, though, the greater the burden of fear that any day I might fall from "the best and the brightest" pedestal on which I perched precariously. Along the way, I began to put more pressure on myself. I no longer needed my parents' and teachers' expectations; I had my own unrealistic expectations of perfection. As ridiculous as it seems now, I became convinced that if I believed in the worst possible outcome, I could only be pleasantly surprised in the end. Apart from being irritating to students who faced challenges in school, this signaled the beginning of a lifetime of negativity that did not serve me well.

My childhood was likely not much worse or better than anyone else's. Yes, I had difficult things to deal with in my home life and at school, but maybe my brain was just wired to be anxious. I developed unhealthy tools to deal with that anxiety, and I continued to use those tools until they caused more problems than they solved."

When I started attending recovery meetings in my mid-forties, a friend told me that for every negative thought, I needed to come up with two positive thoughts. This was absurd. I had been honing my negativity for over thirty years. I was drowning in my struggles; negativity consumed me.

Ultimately, I reached the conclusion that the only way to generate positive thoughts was to suppress the negative ones. Thus began my journey to eliminate my chronic negative thinking. Every time I had a negative thought, I stopped right there and flipped it to make it positive. For example, when I was angry because I was stuck in traffic and concerned about being late, I reframed it; while I was sitting there, I had time to process my mental to-do list. Over time, it worked, but it took a lot of practice. When the weight of anxiety bears down on me, even today, my thoughts still turn towards negativity. It seems almost like it is my default setting, but I know I have the tools to combat that negativity and to turn my day around.

After receiving my cancer diagnosis and deciding to have a bilateral mastectomy, try as I might, the negativity slithered in at all times of day and night. Since I was teaching high school English, it would be fair to assume I would be too busy to dedicate time to being lost in negative thoughts. While students worked diligently, and not so diligently, on their Chromebooks, though, I became teary eyed and hopeless. I prided myself on being tough and part of that involved not crying in front of a room of twenty-eight high school sophomores, so I shut it down, but it continued to sneak up on me. There was no way to stop this cycle; I just needed to walk through the emotions, and that was the last thing I wanted to do.

This time period and these emotional struggles taught me things about people that escaped my notice in the previous four decades of my life. My preoccupation with my cancer diagnosis, the associated decisions, and all the emotions cycling through my head on repeat prevented me from seeing the whole picture, which includes the fundamental goodness of people. And yes, teenagers are people. I am cognizant of the fact that some of you may be parents of teenagers right now and, as such, you may find this difficult to believe. I can assure you they are hiding some of their best qualities from you. Like any good language arts student, I will support my argument with evidence.

The doctors set the date for my surgery on November 21, the Monday before Thanksgiving. The kids would be off school that Thursday and Friday, but experience told me that many students would not come to school at all that week. Some would be hunting; some would take planned family vacations for the holiday; some would have fictional hunting trips and family vacations. Regardless, if I planned to inform my students about my six-week absence, I needed to do it before they were gone. I decided I would tell all of my classes on Thursday, a week before Thanksgiving.

I am a planner, so I outlined ahead of time how I would deliver this message to my classes. We operated on a four-period block schedule, so students attended four ninety-minute classes. This meant that I taught three classes besides my prep period, so I would only need to endure this brand of torture three times.

With three minutes left in each class, as I heard the telltale sound of backpack zippers, I walked to the front of the classroom and scanned the rows until students began to look up from what they were doing. I said, "I need your attention for just a couple of minutes. I am going to be out of school for a bit because of some health issues and I wanted you to hear what is going on from me." All eyes were focused on me now. If only they were that focused when I talked about the structure of an essay.

"I have breast cancer," I continued, "and I will have surgery on Monday. After my surgery, I will be off school for six weeks to recover, but I will be back in January." I delivered this short, matter-of-fact explanation without emotion and when I was finished, I looked at them and smiled in an attempt to convey confidence.

These fifteen- and sixteen-year-olds stared at me—some blankly, some with concern, and a couple with tears in their eyes. Student tears would normally be reason enough for me to provide reassurance to them. That did not follow the script, though, and to be honest, I didn't have the emotional capacity at that moment to reassure anyone else. I just needed to get through this three times without crying. Thankfully, it was time to transition to the next class. As students gathered their things and headed for the door, I thought about the genuine concern of my students. It touched my heart in a way that the response of the adults I talked to about my diagnosis did not.

In the meantime, the staff had all received pink breast cancer awareness shirts. The next morning prior to school, we assembled in the gym wearing our shirts for a photograph. I thought I was ready for this. I had been teaching for sixteen years and it was just another staff picture. The photographer arranged the staff in the shape of a cancer awareness ribbon in the middle of the gym floor, with me in the middle of the ribbon. Seeing staff members wearing those pink shirts and realizing they were standing by me both literally and figuratively was equal parts encouraging and overwhelming. Taking the picture only required about three minutes, but what followed proved to be more challenging. The scene included hugs, promises to pray, and attempts to crack a joke to lighten the mood. I appreciated the fact that many of my colleagues knew me well enough to make the attempt at humor.

As the first bell rang, we scattered to make our way to our first period classes. I nearly sprinted to the bathroom to wipe my tears and get myself together to deal with the chaos of teenagers approaching Thanksgiving Break. The last thing I needed was for students to see me crying in the hallway. It occurred to me, as it had on many occasions lately, how lucky I was to teach here. This community had experienced significant growth. The high school housed eleven hundred students; however, the sense of a small community remained. This work family of mine was wrapping me in their warm embrace, and I loved them for that. I just wondered how I would get through this day without a complete emotional breakdown.

I had concerns about the potential consequences of my announcement to students the previous day. It crossed my mind that there might be questions today. As I started class first period, though, it seemed like business as usual. This was a speech class, and we were in the middle of an informative speech unit. As usual, I referred students to the timeline. They should have their planning guide completed with their thesis and main points, and they should have collected and annotated their sources. Then I gave them some notes to review formal outlining. During work time, students would work on their outline and come to me with questions. This is when I thought kids might approach me to discuss my cancer. I didn't want to shut them down, but my heart raced imagining their questions about my health. What if I could not remain calm and composed and answer them in a professional manner? If I started crying today, I might not stop. No need to worry, though. It turns out that most teenagers don't like emotions any more than I do. They worked as diligently as I had ever seen them work and they approached me with content and outlining inquiries only. I had hit the jackpot. These sophomores were just socially awkward enough to save all of us from having to deal with some big emotions. I was thankful for that.

There were ten minutes between classes. As usual, I used this time to go to the bathroom, fill my water bottle, and chat with colleagues in the hall. When I walked back into my classroom, I stopped short. Each and every student in my Honors English 11 class was wearing pink clothing. They had decorated my old-school chalkboard using pink and white chalk. Messages of love and strength covered the entire board. I couldn't imagine how they had done all of this in ten minutes. I looked out at their smiling faces and with a tentative smile and an unsteady voice, I said, "Okay. Thank you. We are going to take a picture and then we are going to get to work because I am not going to cry today." They laughed nervously, and I took a deep breath, willing away the tears that threatened to fall. I still smile today when I look at this picture. I don't know where those young people are now, but at sixteen years old, they already understood the importance of seemingly small acts of kindness and how impactful they can be. These young people were most definitely "good."

During work time, a boy came up and asked, "Can I go to the bathroom and change back into my other shirt?" I laughed. "Of course you can." I had never felt so loved. These teenage boys loved me enough to put on pink shirts and walk through the hallway with their peers just to lift my spirits. I smiled with gratitude as he left the classroom. I loved my job!

I have spent my entire life operating in a constant state of something I call "manageable" anxiety. This is another way of saying that I stuffed my feelings. I've struggled with asking others for help and I spent my entire life convinced that I am the only one I can depend on. This meant that I "sucked it up" and went through life as though nothing could derail me. Obviously, that didn't always work. Alcoholism knocked me off the rails in 2009, but after some repairs, the train slowly moved forward until this latest obstruction on the track. Two years into sobriety, I had not yet embraced the idea that I had a Higher Power who was in control and who would help me if I let them. And I certainly wasn't ready to ask other people for help. I had this obsessive need to be tough, and a component of that was persuading myself that I could accomplish things without leaning on others. I just needed to pick myself up, brush myself off, and keep moving forward, one step at a time.

Even this stubborn German knew that I could do nothing to help my kids in this building while I was at home recovering from surgery, so I emailed the staff. I needed to thank them for their support. They had already arranged a meal train so I wouldn't need to worry about how to feed my 15- and 16-year-old after my surgery. And in addition to planning the pink ribbon picture that morning, many had stopped by during the day to wish me well and to offer prayers. Although I was terrified about what was to come, these visits presented a welcome diversion from my own thoughts.

Anyone who has struggled with anxiety knows how valuable this is. I've often told friends that "being alone in my head is a very scary place to be." This always gets a chuckle, but it was no joke as I struggled to deal with my cancer diagnosis. One small thought running through my mind could transform into a labyrinth of concerns and I could become ensnared within that maze for days. I appreciated the distraction.

Besides making sure my colleagues understood how grateful I was for their support, I wanted to express my gratitude for the single most important thing they would provide. So I sent an email: "The last thing I want to say is thank you for being here for my kids. They have grown up in this building and some of you have developed close relationships with them over the years. I know they will have good days and not so good days as we navigate this great unknown. I feel better knowing that they have surrogate parents in the building. Thank you in advance for taking care of them here and please reach out with anything you believe I should be aware of. I love you all and I don't know what I would do without my Holmen family." I signed it, picked up my things, and headed out the door for the next six weeks.

Fast forward several weeks. (I will share more about the details of these pretty significant weeks later.) Before Christmas break, I received a message that a student had dropped off a gift in my room. Feeling better, I made a brief visit to the school during break, appreciating the quiet halls. I just wasn't up for polite conversation. When I entered the classroom, I saw a package on my desk. Inside was a fleece tie blanket and a handwritten note left by a student I had never met. She said, "Mrs. Jeske (my name at the time), you don't know me, but I know your daughter, Abbey. My mom had cancer when I was young, and I know how hard it is ... I wanted to do something to help and I know that when my mom was going through her cancer, her blanket always made her feel a little better. I hope this blanket helps you too." I hugged the blanket to my chest with tears in my eyes. This young girl who lost her mom to cancer wanted to do something to help someone she had never even met. Wow! I don't care what anyone says about teenagers; there are some amazing young people out there. I know some adults who could stand to learn a lesson from this young lady. I still have that blanket and it still makes me feel better when I'm having a bad day.

Upon my return to school, there was still one more surprise waiting for me. Empty Bowls is a national program in which artists and craftspeople come together to provide support to those in need. Our high school had been taking part in this program for several years. The ceramics classes threw bowls of all shapes and sizes. Those attending the event purchased a bowl (or several bowls) and they received a soup dinner. It was the perfect winter fundraiser, and the Art Club decided who the recipients of the funds would be each year.

I had attended many times and purchased multiple bowls, but this winter, not feeling up to it, I had not attended. To my surprise, the Art Club had chosen my family as recipients, and at the next assembly, they presented me with a check for $1000. To be honest, I'm sure there were others who were more in need of the money, but I appreciated the fact that the students had thought of us, and I felt so loved. We purchased some food with part of the money and we donated a portion to the local food pantry since we already had more meal train dinners in our freezer than we could eat. Those kids were onto something; it did feel good to give back. I had been doing so much more taking than giving in these weeks, and I was more than happy to pay it forward.

The year moved on, and by June I started feeling more like myself. My hair was growing back, the color was returning to my face, and I had more energy and motivation than I had felt since October. These were the conditions under which I agreed to teach summer school. One speech class, three hours a day, for four weeks. I had done it countless times, but things were different this summer, and not just me. I couldn't believe how naughty these fifteen- and sixteen-year-olds were during class. They were chatty; it seemed to take forever to settle them down to begin a task. One boy insisted on following me around the room asking inane questions: "What if I haven't picked a topic?" "Can I do my demonstration speech on how to avoid giving a speech?" "If I brought you a Snickers Bar, would you let me not give the speech?" I swear I once owned a golden retriever who followed me around less than this boy. They displayed focus during their peers' speeches, and even offered constructive feedback, but beyond that, they were exhausting.

One night, while recounting their behavior to a friend, she said, "They seem like normal teenagers to me." I found myself amid an epiphany. They weren't naughty; they were normal. For the past eight months, the teenagers in this building had walked on eggshells around me, afraid to be themselves, trying to make my life easier. Now things were simply getting back to normal. This was one more piece of evidence that most teenagers are kindhearted, compassionate, and thoughtful. I considered myself blessed to have had the best job in the world, working with good teenagers who I hoped would grow into better, even more gracious adults.

No time is a good time to have cancer, and nothing makes that journey easy. If there is one thing that can make it bearable, though, it is good people doing extraordinary things. Here's what I learned about giving to others. It is not necessary to possess a large sum of money or to have an overwhelming amount of time.

You don't have to be super creative or perform grand gestures. It can be as simple as a symbolic act, like dressing up in pink to show support or going to a fundraiser to buy a bowl. It can be dropping a meal off at someone's house or making a blanket.

Our children (yes, even teens) are miles ahead of the rest of us here. Perhaps it is because their lives are so dependent on their personal relationships. Or maybe it is because they don't see a personal cost to helping others. I am sometimes inclined to pass on signing up for the next fundraiser or the latest meal train because I "just don't have the time." I wonder, though, if that is true or if it is about what adults prioritize. As a high school teacher, almost every time someone asked me what I did for a living, they would follow my answer with a disparaging comment about teenagers. I am here to tell all those doubters: you are wrong; most people are good. Even teenagers. Cancer taught me that.

# Chapter 6

# Cancer Is Isolating

"The loneliest moment in someone's life is when they are watching their whole world fall apart, and all they can do is stare blankly."
F. Scott Fitzgerald, *The Great Gatsby*

I taught high school for twenty-eight long years. I taught all day, interspersing delivery of content with ongoing attempts to maintain control in a classroom of teens with raging hormones and no filters. In between all of that, I responded to emails, attended meetings, and dealt with the onslaught of ever-growing requirements piled on by well-meaning administrators. Google says that the average teacher makes fifteen hundred decisions a day. I call that a conservative estimate, even if we operate on the often-debunked theory that teachers have a forty-hour work-week. In reality, after my eight-hour workday, I went home and did all the other parts of my job that there was no time for during my day. This is when I did my curriculum planning and graded piles of sophomore essays. Then I woke up and did it all over again. It was exhausting. The inner dialogue in my brain never stopped, day or night. There were days when I couldn't imagine feeling more exhausted, but then I received a cancer diagnosis. I was on the verge of a new understanding of exhaustion.

Sometimes fatigue is not about the number of decisions made during the day. I did not need to make fifteen hundred decisions a day related to my cancer, but I found myself alone on the island where those decisions needed to be made. There were no right or wrong answers, and there were no guarantees. Sure, I talked to doctors, my friends, and my partner, but in the end, it was just me. This was my burden, and I never felt as lonely as I did on this journey.

The journey had already been a long one, filled with waiting for answers. First, I had the mammogram, which showed suspicious areas but gave me no answers. Then the ultrasound; still no answers. Then we moved to a biopsy, and we had to wait again. The waiting seemed like the hardest part to me. I have never been a patient person and waiting for answers gave me way too much time to imagine the worst-case scenario. As much as I tried to convince myself that this was likely a false alarm, something just never felt right. Then I received the cancer diagnosis and met with the surgeon. I thought now we would schedule surgery and move into solution mode because we had determined the problem, but first we needed to do an MRI. More waiting. Seriously?! I just needed answers, and I needed someone to tell me what I should do. I didn't want to be an adult. "Adulting sucks," as the millennials are fond of saying. Unfortunately, no matter how much it sucked, there was only one person who could decide what to do—*me*!

I had at long last made the first decision. I would have a bilateral mastectomy. The surgeon would remove both breasts, leaving me board flat for the first time since fourth grade. It would be a double surgery of sorts—three hours for the mastectomy and another three hours to insert the tissue expanders—balloon-like sacs inserted under the skin to help to make a pocket to put the implant into later. Over time, these expanders would reach the desired size, allowing the skin to stretch.

When I woke up from surgery, these expanders would already have some saline in them, beginning this stretching process. Initiating the plastic surgery process simultaneously with the mastectomy was supposed to improve my emotional state by avoiding the sudden realization of a flat chest upon waking up. Based on the information provided by my surgeons, this was considered an outpatient surgery. As a result, I would be discharged on the same day and await the pathology screening results for the tissue taken from my body at home.

My breast surgeon and my plastic surgeon were both exceptional. They explained things to me using language that was within my grasp. Cade came to the early appointments with me and I kept looking at him to help me make decisions, but he wouldn't do that. Instead, he sat back and asked questions. He believed having all the information would enable me to make the best decision for myself. His reticence only made me feel isolated and alone in this battle, and it made me angry. Of course, I didn't tell him that; I just expected him to be my partner in this battle. There was a part of me that knew he was not really invested, and I was afraid I might find out that he was just trying to do "the next right thing" by being here at all.  I expected that being in a relationship would diminish my feelings of solitude, but it didn't. And the more alone I felt, the more scared I became. I just wanted to snap my fingers and get to surgery day, because waiting was hard.

Prior to my surgery date, I continued to go to work, do my job to the best of my ability, and attend my kids' activities. I felt pressure to be strong for everyone around me. When teaching, I remained professional and focused on my students and my curriculum. With my kids, I portrayed a sense of normalcy. I didn't know another way to operate. I grew up learning to be strong; I always took on the role of caring for others and I couldn't allow others to see my vulnerability.

None of this was because I am that selfless; it's because I had created my own personal martyrdom complex. The pressure I felt was of *my* making; these expectations came from me alone. This is not the first time people have accused me of having unreasonable expectations. As a parent, I always expected my kids to do their best. As a teacher, I had a reputation for being a tough grader.

There existed no one I was more critical of than myself, however, and there existed no period that those expectations were as impractical as they were during the cancer season of my life.

Now that I knew I was dealing with cancer, I just wanted to have the surgery and find out if I needed to do chemotherapy. On good days, I had faith in my capacity to handle anything. I saw it as a kind of homework assignment. Tell me what to do and I'll do it. On bad days, I dreaded finding the rest of the answers because the answers I'd received so far had poked holes in my confidence and my resolve.

I convinced myself that every time I got news, it would be worse than the news I had already received. This is what I do. When I have to wait too long, I get trapped in this horrible hamster wheel, and pretty soon I am certain my outcome is going to be so much worse than it actually is. This worst-case scenario thinking is a throwback to the "stinking thinking" from my drinking days and earlier. I wanted someone to help me break out of this thinking, but I was struggling and, as usual, I did that while isolating.

So when I wasn't at school, I was hiding in my bedroom feeling sorry for myself. I convinced myself that I was protecting my kids by not sharing my feelings with them. The reality is that I was emotionally unavailable, and that probably scared them more than anything else that was going on. I didn't have the tools to do anything different at that point in my life, though. I had never been good at emotions. I spent decades using alcohol to numb my feelings, and now that I no longer had that crutch, I wasn't sure how to deal with any of this. I also had no idea how to process what I was feeling. Was I scared? Yup. Was I sad? Sure. Was I angry? Oh yeah. I was pissed as hell! The thing is that it's hard to be mad at cancer. What do you do with that? I had no idea, and I was conscious of the fact that sometimes, during my drinking days, my version of anger was downright scary to others. These are things I was working to change in my life, so instead of releasing angry Angela to the wild, I hid her away from everyone.

The only place that I could be anything close to honest was at my recovery meetings. I understood that if I wasn't honest with someone, I might beat cancer, but there was a high likelihood I wouldn't do it sober. I had been practicing the principles of this program long enough to be aware that if I didn't prioritize my sobriety ahead of everything else, I would lose the things that were important to me. I put in a lot of work to repair relationships with family members, and I had no intention of surrendering the progress I had made. I had been fortunate; I had a high bottom; I had avoided being arrested or incarcerated, and I had maintained my job, my family, and my house. At the same time, though, I had lost all self-respect, descending into self-loathing before I found sobriety, and I couldn't bear to go back there. Or worse. That is why I went to a meeting every day leading up to surgery day. Sometimes I shared and other times I just sat in the room, listened, and cried. I didn't know much, but I knew I didn't want cancer to be a reason to drink.

Looking back, I realize I did not always have to be strong. I had many friends and family members who wanted to be my rock. They wanted me to lean on them and they in no way expected me to be the one in the caretaking role as I struggled to deal with my health and emotions. Everyone is different, though, and I honestly believe that this is what I had to do to cope during this time. Caring for others prevented me from focusing on myself. In part, this is a technique I learned in recovery. When I became too focused on my own thoughts and started perseverating, all I had to do was reach out to another alcoholic, and they would pull me out of my pity party. What I hadn't learned yet is that there is a need for balance in life. I can't sit in a pity party for too long, but I also can't stuff all of my feelings under a blanket of empathy. I had not yet figured out how to ask for or accept help. Cancer is lonely, but it can be far less lonely if we let others in.

At night when I was alone in my room, I let go of all pretense. There was no one there but me, and this is when my thoughts spun out of control. My thoughts were illogical and disjointed. I sobbed until I was gasping, trying to catch my breath. I knew the truth of what I couldn't admit to anyone else. I was scared. Terrified, in fact. What if they couldn't get rid of the cancer? What would happen to my kids? I had told them I would be okay, and I needed that to be true.

I also felt like I was losing my identity. I had never thought myself a vain person; I had never spent a lot of time on clothing, hair, and makeup; I just wasn't that girl. Often, as an adolescent girl, I had wished that I was less well endowed. Now, though, all I could think about was how much I didn't want to be a flat-chested bald woman. My alter ego argued: "So you'd rather be a dead woman with boobs and hair?" Believe me, my logical brain knows how ridiculous my thoughts were, but my emotional brain couldn't think logically. Not then. When I got sober, I had to learn how to walk through my feelings, something I was still learning when I got my diagnosis; now all I wanted was to numb them, but that was no longer an option.

At long last, the week of my surgery arrived. One thing I learned during this journey is that there is no room for modesty when you're facing a bilateral mastectomy. On November 18, 2011, I stood bare-chested in front of my plastic surgeon for my pre-op appointment. He used me as his personal easel, drawing on my chest with purple marker. Then his nurse took pictures from all angles. I was in too much of a fog to worry about my dignity, and that's probably a good thing because standing naked from the waist up covered in purple marker in front of my gorgeous plastic surgeon, dignity wasn't even a word in my vocabulary. All I could do was act as though this wasn't the most awful experience of my life. The surgeon and his nurse tried to make me comfortable, or at least less uncomfortable, but there was nothing that would decrease my anxiety three days before my surgery.

On surgery day, my parents planned to come down to sit with my daughter Abbey, who had decided that she needed to be at the hospital more than she needed to be at school. She and her brother have always dealt with things differently, and he decided he had to go to school. He had three tests that day and an orchestra concert that night, but more importantly, I think it would have been too difficult emotionally for him to be at the hospital all day. I was as relieved that school would distract him as I was that Abbey would have my parents and Cade in the waiting room with her. My older daughter was also coming home from college and it helped me to know that her support system would surround her, too.

The three days leading up to the surgery were a blur. No matter what I was doing, the tears were waiting to fall. I cried at the grocery store and I cried while doing the laundry. Were my shirts even going to fit after my surgery? And why was I even washing these bras that I would never wear again? I held it together when my kids were around, but as soon as I walked into my bedroom and closed the door, the tears flowed. Every night that week, I laid on my bed sobbing into the pillow so the kids wouldn't hear me. I didn't want to make this any worse for them.

My body ached with weariness as night descended upon me. All I wanted to do was sleep. I laid down, sure I would pass out in minutes, only to stare at the ceiling with tears streaming down my cheeks. At some point, when I had cried myself dry, I fell asleep just to wake and do it all over again the next day. Each day, I became increasingly fearful and discouraged. I had put in so much effort to transform my life and now I was being bullied by these small masses concealed deep in my breast tissue. I had encountered bullying in the past, but nothing compared to this. Never had I felt so intimidated. I wanted to scream in my loudest teacher voice: "Fuck you, cancer! Fuck you! I will not let you win!"

# Chapter 7

# Some Lessons Can Only Be Taught by Adversity

"When everything seems to be going against you, remember that the airplane takes off against the wind, not with it."
Henry Ford

Surgery day finally arrived. I wanted the answers the day would provide, but a bilateral mastectomy was a shitty way to get those answers. We headed to the hospital at four in the morning. The doctors planned to start the surgery at seven. I was terrified but trying to hold it together for my family. When I woke up in post-op, I would be forever altered physically and emotionally. In the car, I tried to focus on maintaining a positive attitude for Abbey as I assured her everything would be all right. When we arrived at the hospital, Cade and Abbey sat in the waiting room while the nurses got me "gowned up." The plan was that my parents would be there by the time they brought Cade back so that Abbey didn't have to sit alone.

My focus was centered on breathing and clearing my mind when the nurse brought Cade to pre-op. "Your parents are here," he said.

I nodded, tears glistening in my eyes. I found myself speechless, an uncommon occurrence for me. I wanted Cade to comfort me, but I did not know what he could say that would be comforting.

He looked at me, and, after a moment, he said, "All you need to think about is being here for the next thirty years for your kids."

I am sure he meant for that to be reassuring, but what I wanted him to say in that moment was that he loved me and needed me and everything would be okay once we beat cancer. He was in the room physically, but I felt alone. I knew that he had been prepared to end our relationship before my cancer diagnosis and his response reaffirmed my belief that he would not remain with me once this was over. If he didn't want me, why would anyone else?

In December of 2009, I was in a much different place. I was seven months sober and feeling the "pink cloud" of sobriety. Most days, I couldn't believe how good I felt. I no longer woke up every day thinking about when I could drink. One day after a meeting, I was sitting around chatting. In recovery, we call it fellowship. Anyway, this guy I had seen at a bunch of meetings asked me if I wanted to get a coffee sometime. I felt flattered. Why not? I thought. This guy seemed safe to me, or at least to my sobriety. He was 23 years sober, and I knew from listening to conversations around the club, that I enjoyed his sarcastic sense of humor. On December 31st, we met for coffee and talked for a couple hours. It was easy to talk to him and when it was time to go, he asked if I wanted to go to the sober New Years Eve party with him that night. It was the beginning of the healthiest relationship I had ever been a part of.

There had been so many moments over the past two years when Cade said things that made me feel special. It was the first time I could remember feeling that way. Cade was an alcoholic and an addict. He went to treatment three times before he got clean and sober for good. He said it was a judge telling him to make recovery work or he was going to prison that finally made recovery stick. Since getting sober, he had earned his Graduation Equivalency

Diploma (GED) and a technical college degree. A well-established company had just offered him a great job as an electrician. Lying in bed that night, he smiled at me and said, "I can't believe I'm laying in the house I own with the woman I love. I am so blessed, and it's all because I'm sober." I felt so loved and so lucky in that moment.

Not so long after that, though, we were sitting on the couch at Cade's house when he said, "I'm questioning whether we really have anything in common." This was a year into our relationship, and it was the first time he had said anything like this. I just stared at him. I had not seen this coming.

"Are you trying to break up with me?" I asked, puzzled.

"I guess maybe that is what I'm saying."

I latched onto the fact that he seemed so hesitant to say it directly, and I convinced myself that he wasn't sure. I begged him to give us another chance and he eventually agreed. I'm guessing that at this point he was already chatting with other women when he wasn't with me, and this started a spiral of insecurity that fed into my issues with low self-esteem.

Everyone in recovery tells newcomers that it's a bad idea to get into a relationship until you've been sober for at least a year, and it is bad practice for someone with significant sobriety – say 23 years, for example – to start dating someone who is newly sober. I was sure we were the exception, though. And as I laid in this pre-op room, we had been together for nearly two years.

"Hon, how are you doing?" Cade asked, taking my hand in his.

Suddenly, I was back in the hospital room, with negative thoughts racing through my brain. What if something went wrong in surgery? Was there any possibility Cade would want to stay with the hideous, deformed person I was about to become? How was I going to take care of my kids after surgery? They deserved better than this. No amount of breathing or focusing on other things seemed to help.

Before too long, the pre-op nurse appeared in the room. "Hi. My name is Amy and I'm going to get you ready for surgery." There is nothing I hated more than when people gave me that sad look of pity. Relief washed over me as she began walking me through the customary pre-surgery checklist, but then out of nowhere she strayed from her prepared script. "I had breast cancer a couple years ago," she began. "The next year will be the worst year of your life," she continued, tearing up. What the hell was she doing? I don't know what she said after that; I was in shock. I looked at Cade, stunned and mortified, and as she turned to the computer, I mouthed, "Get her the fuck out of here." I'm not sure what happened, but Cade stepped out of the room for just a minute and a different nurse came into the room. Amy left and that's the last I saw of her.

To this day, I cannot understand why anyone would think a nurse who is still struggling emotionally with their own cancer battle should prepare someone for a bilateral mastectomy. Furthermore, how was it even possible for her to think that what she said to me was in any way reassuring? Perhaps she believed I would find solace in having someone in the room who understood, and that could have been true if she hadn't insisted on forewarning me about the upcoming dreadful year right before my surgery. Here's a tip if you ever find yourself talking to someone who is about to have their boobs cut off. If you can't share your experience without being the angel of doom and gloom, maybe just don't talk at all. Sometimes silence truly is the better answer.

The next thing I remember is waking up over six hours later in the most excruciating pain I have ever felt in my life. I had experienced surgeries prior to this, and I have experienced surgeries since. I have always felt like I was in recovery for a hot minute and then was on my way. This time was different. My pain was beyond control. The initial plan involved dedicating three hours to the removal of my breasts, followed by another three hours for placing expanders and injecting saline, then an hour or two in recovery, and finally, making my way home. If that sounds ridiculous, that's because it is. To the best of my knowledge, a mastectomy is no longer an outpatient surgery, but in 2011, apparently the insurance companies called the shots and those companies were run by men who only conceptualized boobs as something created for their pleasure. At any rate, I can tell you unequivocally that sending people home following this surgery is not a great idea.

At some point, the nurses in the recovery room moved my bed to another area because they needed the room. It looked like they might have to admit me. I couldn't wiggle my toes without uttering something between a whimper and a moan. I'm not sure how many pain meds they put in my IV, but the meds seemed to have no effect on the pain. Going through labor and delivery was a breeze compared to this. Fortunately, I drifted in and out of consciousness. That single factor prevented me from being overwhelmed by constant pain. At one point, I remember hearing my mom tell them, "My daughter has the highest pain threshold of anyone I know. If she says she can't go home, she needs to be admitted." In the end, that is what happened.

In the meantime, though, my daughters were in the waiting room, and I can't imagine what they were going through. They expected to see me after surgery, and when that still had not happened, I'm sure they were scared. It turns out, they were busy posting updates for my friends and family.

Before my surgery, I made the decision that I didn't want to explain every step of my journey numerous times as I kept people updated. I resolved the issue by opening a Caring Bridge account and writing all the updates there. That way, people could log in, read the updates, and even share their positive thoughts for me and the kids. The day of surgery, I knew my girls needed to feel like they were doing something, so I asked them to provide updates on the account. To this day, reading those updates brings tears to my eyes. Here is a glimpse, written on November 21, 2011, by my girls.

Hi everyone! It is Rae and Abbey. Just a quick update. The doctor just came in and mom was out of surgery. He says we should be able to see her in about an hour :) Everything went great, and they found NO cancer in her lymph nodes. We just want to thank everyone for all their support and prayers through this time.

It means more than you know to all of us. —Rae and Abbey

We should be able to see mom soon. She woke up in a lot of pain, so they are addressing that first before we can see her. Hopefully, I can see her before I have to head to Winona. —Rae

"Hey all... I had to leave for Winona before I could see mom. Abbey has been texting me,

though, and I can go see her tonight if she comes home. —Rae

So it sounds like Mom may be spending the night in the hospital. I will update you all when I hear more from Abbey. —Rae

Hi all! I finally got to see mom tonight. She is spending the night at Gunderson, but she should go home tomorrow. One of the first things my mom said when I saw her was that Tim and Autumn were there to see her in recovery. My grandma told me something tonight that really got to me. She said when Tim left the room he cried because he has never seen mom be anything but strong and it was really hard to see her in one of her weakest moments. My mom is one of the strongest people I know and even though she is weak now, it is her strength and the strength of all of you reading and cheering her on that will get her through this. Together, we will get past this. —Rae

It has been over twelve years and reading the entries written by my kids still leaves a lump in my throat. For the most part, that lump comes from unresolved guilt over something that was beyond my control. That guilt is irrational, but it is my visceral reaction every single time I read the entries. When someone has cancer, our concern is for them. The truth is, though, that cancer is a family disease. My cancer impacted everyone who cared about me and everyone who counted on me. It transformed my kids' lives forever, and as much as I wish there was something I could have done to change that, it is the reality for so many families. All we can do is to navigate it one day at a time, using the strategies at our disposal. There are as many ways to do this as there are victims of this disease. My story is just one example of one flawed individual making their way through this awful disease.

# Chapter 8

---

# Strength Doesn't Always Look Like Taking a Deep Breath

"Our strength grows out of our weakness. The indignation
which arms itself with secret forces does not awaken until we
are pricked and stung and sorely assailed."
Ralph Waldo Emerson

My bilateral mastectomy was a planned outpatient surgery, but ultimately medical wisdom prevailed over insurance company directives and my doctors opted to admit me overnight. Once I was settled in a room and pretty doped up on painkillers, Dr. Garett came in to check on me. I had four drain tubes—two dangling from each armpit. He frowned a bit when he looked to see how they were draining. There was more fluid in the tubes than he anticipated. I had no idea what that meant, but even the slightest movement of my arms took my breath away, leaving me in tears. Dr. G showed Cade how to check the tubes and empty them and told us they would keep an eye on it overnight. We emptied 400 cubic centimeters of liquid in eight hours. Prior to my surgery,

I had no clue how much 400 centimeters was, but it turns out it's a lot.

By morning, the drainage did slow, but while too much nasty fluid draining from your body after surgery is bad, it is just as bad when virtually none is draining. Dr. Garett was concerned I might have a hematoma, so we headed back to the operating room. This surgery was nowhere near as traumatizing. He went in, removed the clot, and by noon I was back in my room. I guess it's a good thing they kept me overnight.

I spent the afternoon trying to get off IV pain meds so I could go home. By eight o'clock, I had transitioned to taking Lortabs for pain and Flexeril for muscle spasms. The nurse said as soon as I was able to walk to the end of the hallway, they would discharge me.

From a young age, I concealed my weaknesses behind a facade of strength, and it frustrated me that others could see me weak now. As long as the world believed I was tough and in control, I felt safe. For that reason alone, I was determined to go home that day. Maybe my post-op recovery was beyond my control, but I was not accepting defeat. In retrospect, I probably should have stayed another night, but my ego wouldn't allow it. "Let's go!" I said as Cade helped me struggle to my feet. This was no easy task since I couldn't use my arms to get up, but I was determined. Once on my feet, I shuffled a couple steps at a time, stopping and taking slow, deep breaths to get the pain under control. Cade said, "You don't have to do this; you can stay another night if you need to." I shook my head. I needed to be home, and my kids needed that too. We all needed some sort of stability, and I was sure I would find it in my house.

At this point in my cancer journey, I thought being weak was the worst thing I could be. As I traveled farther down this road, though, I realized the problem was how I defined strength and weakness. Sure, physically I was struggling and there would be many moments of emotional struggle during this journey, but the same thing that makes us feel weak can also expose our strength. Together, my kids and I were stronger than we knew.

Strength of character cannot be taught, but it can be developed. This includes things like how deeply we love; having the ability to retain our sense of humor in the face of difficulty; the ability to persevere, be resilient, and walk with courage; and developing a perspective that allows us to treat others with humanity. That strength and stability can exist wherever we are. It is about the people, not the location. Together, my kids and I grew and learned. We were all scared, but we held each other up when we needed to, and we knew we had each other even when no one else understood what we were dealing with. We would leave this journey forever changed, but I would argue that we were changed for the better. My kids are kind, compassionate, and resilient adults today, and I am a survivor.

Sometimes our view of our own strength and weakness is less than objective. Today, I can't believe I survived my cancer not only physically, but emotionally as well. From the outside, it may have looked like I was weak, but the journey through cancer is the second hardest thing I've ever done, right behind gaining and maintaining sobriety, and today I understand that it's okay to say I am proud and grateful for the strength to make both journeys.

The walk to the end of that hospital hallway was interminable, and I still had to make it back to the room. I wasn't sure I could do it, no matter how determined I was. I did make it, at last, and looking at Cade, I asked, "Can we please go home now?"

"Of course we can, hon," he said in response.

I was still unable to lift my arms at all. This made everything difficult, starting with getting dressed. As Abbey and Cade helped me, my eyes filled with tears, and I grimaced in pain. I refused to give up, though; I'm nothing if not stubborn.

The next step was moving from the bed to the wheelchair. It was impossible for me to use my hands to push myself off the bed, and my family was unable to aid in lifting me with my arms. Somehow, we made it happen, only to have to transfer me from the chair to the car when we got downstairs. I felt every bump of that car ride home, and I wiped the tears from my cheeks as they fell, attempting to conceal them. I was trying to protect my kids. I knew they would be worried if they knew how much pain I was still in, and they had worried enough.

The throbbing pain through my chest and back intensified again as I walked through my front door, folding my arms close to my stomach to ease the spasms in my chest. I looked back and forth from the stairs to Cade. Why hadn't I built a ranch-style home instead of this split level? In front of me were steps going up and steps going down. I couldn't lean on the railing because that would require using my arms and I didn't have the strength to climb the stairs without the help the railing could provide.

First, we thought maybe I should sit down and scoot up backwards. My limbs quivered with weakness, and I was unable to rely on my core muscles post-surgery. Time for Plan B. I would make my way up the steps with Cade behind me as a spotter of sorts, his hands on my hips. Abbey and Hunter stood in front of me acting as my cheerleaders. "You can do it, Mom."

It had been all I could do to walk down that flat hospital hallway, and now I needed to lift myself up twelve steps. The intensity of my pain escalated again, but mostly I was physically exhausted. One step at a time, I made my way up the stairs. At every single step, I took a break to catch my breath and get my pain under control. Looking back, this moment seems like a metaphorical representation of my recovery from alcoholism. I wanted to get past one step and onto the next, but even after I completed the previous step, I knew there was still a lot of work remaining.

"I'm sorry. I know I'm taking forever."

"You're doing great," Cade said. "We will go as slow as you need to go." I knew he was lying, but I appreciated it.

When I reached the top of the stairs and saw my recliner, I breathed a sigh of relief. We already knew this was where I would sleep because there was no way I could get into and out of bed. Suddenly, my eyes filled with tears of frustration as I realized all over again how helpless I was. I hated this. It seemed like there was a defeat waiting at every turn. Was anything ever going to feel right again?

Cade showed me the log sheet he had made to track my meds. This is where we would track the amount and frequency with which I was taking my pain killers. I had never been addicted to pills, but as a precautionary measure, we agreed to keep a close eye on my opioid consumption. Such is the life of an addict. It turned out to be a good idea because my brain was pretty foggy over the next couple days and I'm not sure I would have remembered when I had last taken pain meds.

The previous two days hadn't gone as planned, but I was in my house now with the people I cared most about. All I wanted was to sit down and close my eyes. Hunter and Cade helped me into the recliner, and Abbey helped me put my feet up and gave me a blanket. There was no graceful way to sit down, as my arms were useless to me. It was anything but pretty. As I flopped into my chair, taking a break to wait for this wave of pain to pass, I stopped, staring straight ahead, tears filling my eyes again, but this time for a different reason. The view in front of me was breathtaking. While I was in surgery, a good friend had put up my Christmas tree and decorated it in pink lights and ribbons. It was beautiful. This would be the most unconventional Christmas of my lifetime. The tree was a beautiful representation of the strength I was not feeling at that moment. The last twenty-four hours had felt so dark, but the bright pink lights were a welcome sight. And I don't even like pink.

# Chapter 9

# Change Your Attitude, Change Your Life

"If you can't change your fate, change your attitude."
Amy Tan

I couldn't imagine what I had to be thankful for when I woke up on the 24th of November—three days after my surgery. Abbey headed to her dad's house for Thanksgiving, while Hunter went to work at his retail job. I found myself seated in a chair alone, gazing at pink ribbons and lights, tears filling my eyes, feeling sorry for myself. I called a friend in recovery, and she did what recovery friends do for each other. She told me I needed to "get off the pity pot." It is exactly what I needed; I needed someone to remind me of the things that got me sober. My sobriety provided a focus I had used in the past to get out of my head and stop feeling sorry for myself, and I needed to get back to that type of healthier thinking.

When I hung up the phone, I sat down and made a gratitude list. It was one of the longest gratitude lists I have ever made. I had an abundance of people to be grateful for; so many people had been so kind. How could I not be grateful for that? My logical brain embraced the feeling of gratitude, but as I looked at the list it just made me sad. It's not that I wasn't grateful for my army of supporters; I was deeply appreciative. I just couldn't see how I was supposed to move through this. Tears fell on my list even as I tried to cling to any feeling of gratitude. I was still waiting for an update from the surgeon regarding the pathology report, but we did know there was no cancer in my lymph nodes and he assured me that was excellent news. Now sobbing, I added that to the list.

Making a gratitude list had been key to my recovery from alcoholism, but the relief was rarely immediate. It did give me the time, space, and permission to feel. The emotions that I kept so securely behind lock and key all came to the surface as I continued writing. I wrote down the last couple of things on the list, and relaxed back into my recliner. I was physically and emotionally exhausted. I prayed: "God grant me the serenity to accept the things I cannot change, the courage to change the things I can, and the wisdom to know the difference." This prayer had gotten me through so many tough days in early sobriety and there was no reason it couldn't get me through this struggle as well. I couldn't change the fact that I had cancer and needed a mastectomy to get rid of it. I could change my attitude about this battle, though. There were so many people in this world who were sicker than me and who had less support than I did. I could tell myself, I may not have breasts anymore, but I am still here, at least for today.

Determined to change the trajectory of my attitude and refocus my day, I looked at the movies next to my chair. A good friend told me I should watch something funny during my recovery to keep my spirits up, so I had purchased the *Big Bang Theory* on DVD. On Thanksgiving Day, all by myself, I started watching season 1, episode 1. I didn't think I had it in me, but I laughed. I actually laughed out loud. And suddenly I felt my heavy mood lift just a bit.

If I could give one piece of life advice, it would be to laugh as often as you can. Find what is uplifting and funny, and laugh. Find people who make you smile and laugh with them. Find what you can laugh at within yourself, and laugh at that, too. It will not always be easy, and sometimes it will be damn difficult, but laughter can heal you both physically and emotionally, and it is nearly impossible to be upset while you are laughing.

It had now been three days, and I continued to be in considerable physical pain. What made it even more challenging was the increased sense of isolation. Not a single person I talked to knew how it felt to be me right now. Several friends came over to my house and, naturally, my kids and Cade were present, but none of that helped improve my state of mind. And things were about to take another turn.

The day after Thanksgiving, Dr. Lancaster called with the complete pathology report. Before the surgery, we were already aware of the presence of three tumors and several areas of concern. Now he had more answers. The largest tumor measured 1.4 millimeters. This turned out to be positive news because it indicated that all the tumors were categorized as small. Pathology discovered eleven tumors in the right breast, and all eleven turned out to be cancerous. There were eleven freaking tumors in *one* boob! It became evident that mastectomy had been the right decision. It was a great relief that the preliminary report had been correct; there was no cancer in my lymph nodes.

The pathology report's final point discussed the proximity of the nearest cancer to the margins of the removed tissue. The proximity of one tumor to the edge suggested the possibility of cancer cells spreading to the skin surrounding the tumor. There were three options. First, we could do nothing at this time; that was terrifying to me. Second, we could do more limited surgery, to remove more tissue to send to pathology; the thought of more surgery was not appealing either. Finally, they could do radiation prior to reconstruction, and then do chemotherapy after that. Staring down these choices, I found myself on the precipice of a panic attack.

When we talked about the plan prior to surgery, there was no mention of the possibility of radiation. I was to have surgery, reconstruction, and maybe chemotherapy. Of course, I was aware that we wouldn't have a definite understanding of the treatment plan until after surgery, but I had convinced myself that the plan would be reduced, not increased. I felt tears stinging the back of my eyes. Dr. L told me that no recommendation was being made right now. The next step was to meet with the surgeon, the medical oncologist, and the radiation oncologist. They would each give me their recommendation based on their medical expertise, and I could consider that to help me make yet another medical decision. I sighed. That was the last thing I wanted to do right now.

I absent-mindedly clicked my pen as I listened in frustration to the surgeon. I had hoped to hear that he had gotten all the cancer and no more treatment was necessary. Now it sounded like I might need both radiation and chemotherapy. I wanted to cry. I already had my boobs cut off; wasn't that enough?! Depending on the outcome, it might be even longer before we were able to do the reconstruction. I know it probably seems like I was focused on the wrong thing, but I just wanted to feel whole again, and reconstruction was the only way for that to happen. I couldn't wait another six months to even begin that process, to look at myself in the mirror without being repulsed by the reflection I saw staring back at me. How could anyone else look at me when I couldn't even stand to look at myself?

Every day I woke up hoping for improvement, but instead I felt like a semitruck had run over me, backed up, and run over me again. I was aware that I had so much to be grateful for, but I felt helpless. I hated having to depend on other people. It took every ounce of my strength to simply stand up from my chair. I wanted to sleep in my bed, but I couldn't imagine how I would get up in the morning. I could not focus long enough to even read a book. I wanted to go Christmas shopping, but that was not something I had the stamina to do.

Out loud, I said to myself, "Stop, already." Once more, I reminded myself that there were countless individuals in this world who had experienced far greater hardships than me. I knew this intellectually, yet all I wanted was to curl up in a ball and feel sorry for myself. This was especially true today. The news from the surgeon had set me back and now I was struggling both physically and emotionally. Why couldn't I get just one break? What kind of God puts people through this crap? My already tenuous faith was being tested again, and I wasn't sure I could hold on; I wasn't even sure I wanted to. Part of my recovery from alcoholism had been centered on the belief in some sort of higher power. Right now, that was in jeopardy and without meetings, I worried my sobriety might be in jeopardy too.

Prior to my surgery, I attended a meeting almost every day. My favorite by far, though, was my Saturday morning meeting and the first Saturday after surgery I felt the need to go to a meeting, but there was no way I could go to one; I was still fettered to my recliner. I missed my recovery friends, though, and I missed the peace that I experienced when I walked through the doors of a meeting. In the end, I took another nap and then prayed for strength and optimism. I continued praying and hanging on for dear life.

Several visitors came to see me over the next few days. It had been slightly more than a week since surgery, so I suppose it was inevitable—that barrage of emotions overlapping one another like the waves at high tide. I was riding the wave, clutching onto my surfboard tightly, afraid that releasing my grip could prevent me from getting back on the board. Everyone who visited told me I needed to hang on and the ride would eventually get easier. Here's the problem. None of those people knew that. Not my family. Not my friends. Not the doctors. "Have you been through it? Then shut up. Just shut up!" I wanted to scream. I wasn't upset with them. I was just upset. I didn't know who I was anymore; I didn't feel like anything was ever going to be okay again. If I remembered this more clearly, I'm sure I would see that I did not treat any of those well-meaning people the way they deserved to be treated. If you're one of them, consider this a long overdue apology. Looking back, I'm certain I was depressed. I didn't know what to do about it though, so I watched another couple episodes of *Big Bang Theory* and then I let the painkillers kick in and closed my eyes.

A couple of days later, the sun popped out from behind the clouds a bit. I woke up with a sense of well-being, and I could *almost* shower without assistance. Most things seemed a little easier. My friend Jamie stopped over, and I walked to the end of my street with her. Later, I went out and got the mail. Overall, I was out of my chair much more than I had been since my surgery. Mom came down and did some cleaning for me and it was nice to visit with her. Hunter and Abbey both stayed at home, and Rae and her roommate paid a short visit. It was a nice day, and I smiled genuinely for the first time since surgery. All the conversation and laughter may have been too much, though, as I was more exhausted and sorer than I had been in several days.

Once everyone left, and I was alone with my thoughts again, I hit another emotional wall. Up until this point, my efforts were solely focused on my physical struggles. Today I felt better physically, but emotionally I couldn't help but feel broken and defective. I had lost part of my identity. And no, I don't mean to imply that I thought I was nothing more than a pair of boobs. The loss of my breasts made it difficult for me to see myself as attractive or worthy of anyone else's attention, though. I am certain that it all played a role in the grieving process, but it felt awful, and I just wanted to get past this.

Cade told me, "We will beat this no problem. You didn't have anything planned for winter anyway, and we had an awesome summer vacation." I appreciated the positive spin, and his presence was invaluable in helping me to see it from another perspective. The challenge arose from my constant thoughts about a night several months earlier, during a conversation about a friend of mine who underwent breast reduction surgery.

"I get it," I'd said. "Some women have horrible back pain from carrying the weight. The surgery is about more than cosmetics."

"No worries," he'd responded, joking. "I'll help you carry them."

The irony of the situation lies in the fact that a few months later, I wouldn't have a choice in the matter. And now I was left feeling like that's what I was to him, just a vessel to carry a nice pair of tatas. At that moment, I was overwhelmed by feeling unattractive and broken. Throughout my life, I've consistently grappled with believing that I am deserving of love and attention, and the present circumstances only served to reinforce my flawed mindset. Starting in elementary school, my classmates, mostly the boys, made fun of me. It started because I was tall and uncoordinated, but over the years it just bounced from one thing to another. I felt bullied all the way through school, and most of it was related to my appearance. Somewhere along the line, my own thoughts took over for my childhood bullies, and all these years later, I couldn't help feeling like the only reason any man would want to be with me was because I had nice boobs. And now that wasn't even true. I began to see a connection between my low self-esteem and my ability to accept help from others. My whole life I believed that it was my responsibility to fix whatever was wrong in my life. The problem was that this might just be too big for me to fix on my own.

During the six weeks I spent recovering from surgery, I came to realize that while cancer does present a physical battle, the psychological struggle is the hardest part. I grappled with the challenges of losing my independence physically and with the belief that I would never be enough again—for others or for myself. I simply wanted to feel complete, and I wasn't sure that would ever happen.

Another aspect of my struggle was the sensation that I was a horrible parent. I couldn't shake the feeling that I shouldn't have to lean on my kids; they should be able to lean on me. My daughter was fifteen years old, and she was making my meals, making sure I took my meds, emptying my drain tubes, and helping me shower. She was my primary caretaker, and I knew this was in all likelihood going to affect her emotionally for the rest of her life. I wished every day that we had another option.

I can't help thinking now about how many other people are in a similar situation, or worse. What if my kids had been little? How would I ever have managed? Or what if it was just me? I had never even considered those scenarios. In fact, I hadn't really stopped to think at all about people who receive a tough diagnosis like cancer until it was me. It's amazing how we exist inside our own privilege. I never thought about these things because I was lucky to have never had them touch my life—not really. Yes, my grandmother had breast cancer, but I was well insulated from that by my parents. To be fair, I have led a blessed life compared to others.

It was when I was feeling stuck in this depression that I made the decision that I would remind myself regularly that many people have it worse than I do; I no longer wanted to walk through life focused on myself and my struggles. Everybody we meet is going through things we know nothing about. We can stop judging others and instead treat them with empathy and maybe, just maybe, we will be doing a little to make their journey easier. This is what I was determined to do. I would face the rest of this journey with gratitude for what I had rather than feeling sorry for myself for what I had lost. I wouldn't do this perfectly, but my goal was "progress, not perfection."

# Chapter 10

# It's Okay to Ask Questions

"If you don't understand, ask questions. If you're uncomfortable about asking questions, say you are uncomfortable about asking questions and then ask anyway."
Chimamanda Ngozi Adichie, *Americanah*

"Hello, Angela. This is Dr. Lancaster." I was shocked to hear my surgeon's voice on the other end of the phone line at six thirty on a Friday evening. "I wanted to give you a quick update, and I didn't want to make you wait until Monday." Have I mentioned what an amazing human being my surgeon is? He called me personally on a Friday night instead of making me wait until Monday. Most specialists never pick up a phone to call a patient, much less call them outside of business hours. Regardless of what else was happening with my health, I was completely confident that I had the best surgeon possible.

"We have a cancer panel consisting of surgeons, oncologists, chemotherapy specialists, and radiologists," he continued. "We meet every Friday to discuss complicated cases such as yours. What makes your case complicated is that none of your tumors are large. If they had been, we would recommend radiation, but in your case, the largest of the tumors was 1.4 cm. The issue is that you had eleven tumors in one breast, so we were unsure whether we should treat them as eleven small tumors or as one large tumor." That made sense to me, but I held my breath, hoping that he was not about to tell me that I was going to have to go through radiation as well as chemotherapy.

"There was also one tumor that I didn't get a clear margin on, so there is a concern that there could be cancer we don't know about in the skin surrounding the area. The team agreed that if I believed I could perform another surgery and get that clear margin, we could forego radiation. I am confident that I can do that."

There it was. I would have more surgery. Then, four to eight weeks after that surgery, I would begin chemo and that would take four months. Four to eight weeks after that, if the surgery found more cancer, I would have radiation. Radiation would delay the placing of the implants, and it also carried with it a high risk that my body might reject the expanders that were already in place for reconstruction. This would mean an infection and yet more surgery. The good news, though, was that if Dr. Lancaster's surgery detected no more cancer, I would not need radiation at all.

"Will I still need to have chemotherapy if you get a clear margin?"

Dr. L told me I should discuss that with Dr. Adebayo, the medical oncologist, so a couple days later, I was again sitting in my oncologist's office feeling on edge and more than a little sick to my stomach.

Dr. Adebayo entered the room with a huge smile on his face. I never saw Dr. Adebayo without a grin that went from ear to ear, and that smile matched his personality, which I can only describe as bubbly. I'm not sure if this was genuine or his idea of professionalism. All I know is that while I didn't dislike him, from the first time I met him, I found his bubbly nature to be off-putting."

Angela, how are you today?"

"I'm okay. I'm just hoping for some answers today."

Dr. Adebayo has a thick accent. I had to lean forward in my chair, reading his lips and facial expressions as I listened to the words he was saying. I found that the visual cues helped when I couldn't quite understand something he said.

"Okay. Well, let us get started then. The cancer is more aggressive than we thought and you are only forty-six years old." He paused, waiting to see if I had a comment. I did not.

"We have an excellent computer program where we input your information." He turned the computer screen so I could see it and pointed out where he had entered the stage of my cancer (stage 1), how aggressive the cancer was, and my age. He continued, "If you were eighty, we wouldn't recommend chemotherapy, but because you are only forty-six and you have a lot of life left, this is sort of your insurance policy."

I didn't know what to say, and I didn't think I could speak at that moment anyway. I struggled with his accent, but what he was saying was clear. I needed to undergo chemotherapy despite their belief that they had eliminated all the cancer. As I look back at this conversation, I realize this was a recommendation, not a mandate, but at the time I did not understand that. He was a specialist, and I had never been taught to question specialists. I knew nothing about cancer. Not really. The specialist told me a computer said I should have chemotherapy, so I was going to have chemotherapy.

Having cancer has taught me all kinds of things about doctors, hospitals, and medicine. One thing I learned is that patients assume doctors have all the answers and we don't always ask the questions we should ask. We rarely question what we are being told. If that were not the case, I probably would have said, "Okay. But if Dr. Lancaster got all the cancer, why do I need to have chemo?" or "What are my chances of cancer recurring without the insurance policy of chemotherapy?" I didn't ask either question. I believed, as so many of us do, that my oncologist was the specialist and I wasn't, so I didn't question his expertise. In fact, I didn't discover until I was writing this book that he had just completed his Hematology and Oncology Fellowship one year prior to the year of my diagnosis. I'm not saying he wasn't qualified, but shouldn't I have known that? I googled everything else.

If I had asked questions, maybe I would have said no to the pumping of poison through my veins. Maybe twelve years later, I wouldn't have peripheral neuropathy in my feet; maybe my veins wouldn't fight the phlebotomists every time I go in for bloodwork; and maybe I wouldn't have the fatigue and brain fog that still plagues me almost daily. Or maybe I wouldn't be here to complain about these things at all. I will never know how one simple question might have changed the trajectory of my journey.

I'm not saying I shouldn't have had chemotherapy and I'm not saying Dr. Adebayo wasn't a good doctor. What I'm saying is that there are not many situations in which we are willing to walk blindly through a fire simply because a person we barely know tells us to. I was a high school teacher for twenty-eight years and I spent a good share of that time defending my professional judgment to people who knew far less about education than I did. It never once occurred to me that people should just accept what I told them because I had an education degree, yet we think that somehow a medical degree is different; somehow *that* degree means the person holding it is more than just another person doing the best job they can in their chosen field.

All of my doctors were amazing and again I am not saying they gave me poor advice. My intent in telling my story is to share what I learned, and one big thing I learned is that I am the patient; it is my body; and I have a right to ask questions. I am no longer a wallflower when I go to a doctor's appointment. I ask for what I need and if I do not feel like my doctors are hearing me or responding to my needs, I find a different doctor. I have heard too many horror stories to just accept the possibility of poor healthcare. Maybe I would have learned this by now with or without cancer, but my experiences with cancer certainly sped up that learning curve.

"Let me tell you a little about what to expect," Dr. Adebayo continued. "There will be eight chemotherapy treatments two weeks apart. The first four treatments will be the medications

Adriamycin and Cytoxan." He handed me information sheets on the two medications. "These treatments will last six hours each." He assured me they had several anti-nausea meds that should help prevent vomiting, but I should expect to be fatigued because of lower blood counts. He also said I would begin to lose my hair after about two weeks. He looked at me and said cheerfully, "Don't worry. Your hair will grow back." Then he turned his attention to Cade and his balding head. "I can't promise you the same thing," he quipped. We both laughed, grateful for the momentary lightening of the mood.

After those first four treatments, I would have four treatments of a medication called Taxol, again two weeks apart. Again, he handed me an information sheet. "You can participate in a clinical trial and then you will have eight smaller doses of Taxol one week apart. This would lighten the side effects a bit."

I wasn't trying to be a martyr, but I could not afford to take more time off of work. I had no idea if I would be able to work through chemotherapy or if I would need to take more time off, and I had already used more than six weeks of sick leave for my surgery. The fact that I needed chemotherapy at all hit me hard. I just wanted to get back to "normal" as soon as possible.

"The other thing about the clinical trial is the potential positive outcomes for other women as it benefits research."

I have always been one to jump to help others and tears filled my eyes as the guilt washed over me. Maybe I was being selfish if I didn't do the trial. Cade, seeing my reaction, stepped in, though, and said, "That's great, but I'm not interested in what's best for other women; I'm interested in what's best for Angela. For a moment, I felt just a little less alone.

All I could say when I sat down to write a CaringBridge entry at the end of the day was, "Please start collecting hats and scarves for me. I have never seen my head bald, but somehow, I don't think it will be pretty. Keep those thoughts and prayers coming - I need each and every one of them. I, for my part, will continue to work to stay in my 24-hour universe. It is difficult right now, but it is my goal every morning when I wake up." This had been one of the rough days.

# Chapter 11

# Fear Is Sometimes Worse Than Reality

"We suffer more often in our imagination than we do in reality.... He suffers more than necessary, who suffers before it is necessary."
Seneca

The kids and I ushered in 2012 with little fanfare and no New Year's resolutions. Surviving chemotherapy just does not seem like a resolution in keeping with the spirit of a New Year's celebration. In just a few days, I would head to the clinic for my first chemotherapy treatment. Once again, I felt disabled by fear of the unknown. When I attended my first AA meeting in 2009, I knew what to expect; I mean, I had seen it in movies. Once more, when I visited the hospital for my bilateral mastectomy, I felt confident in my knowledge of what to expect based on the information shared by others. Though I was incorrect on both counts, now I needed to undergo chemotherapy, and the little knowledge I possessed was terrifying.

Then Dr. Adebayo called with the treatment plan at the beginning of December. The team had decided I would undergo chemotherapy as the initial treatment, followed by the subsequent surgery, hoping to validate their belief that radiation was unnecessary. "We will begin chemotherapy around December 15. "Had I heard that right? It was even more difficult for me to understand his thick accent on the phone.

"December 15?" I asked.

"Yes. The 15th of December."

Like hell you will, I thought. I still had two drain tubes, so I didn't think that was going to happen anyway, but it didn't matter because I wasn't starting chemo before Christmas. I would not do that to my kids. There was nothing they would do at the clinic now that they couldn't do after Christmas. I refused to allow cancer to dictate everything in my life.

"I would prefer to wait to do the first treatment after Christmas," I countered politely. This was the first time I stood up to any of the doctors and it had nothing to do with my health but everything to do with my family.

Dr. Adebayo said, "Okay, Angela. The nurse will call to get that scheduled."

A week later, I was down to one drain tube when the nurse called to tell me what was next and to get everything on the calendar. "Dr. Adebayo has scheduled a heart scan for next Monday, and your port placement and first chemotherapy treatment will take place on December 15," she began.

What part of "no" did that man not understand? I told him I was not starting chemo before Christmas, and I meant it. He planned to enjoy a pleasant Christmas with his family, and I intended to celebrate Christmas with mine as well. I clarified to the nurse that there was still a drain tube in place. She said they only need a couple of days' notice, and the tube only has to be out for a couple of days in order to start treatment. Filled with frustration, I said, "Well, that really doesn't matter because, as I told the doctor, I am not starting chemotherapy before Christmas. My kids deserve a nice Christmas after enduring everything they have already been through."

My experience has been that nurses are much better listeners than doctors, especially specialists, and this one was no exception. She heard what I said and I'm sure she caught the emotion in my voice as well. "No worries," she said. "We will make that work."

They scheduled the heart scan for the next Monday and port placement three days later, but no treatment until after the first of the year. She finished by explaining to me the details of what a day of chemo would entail for me.

On a typical treatment day, I would arrive at the clinic at 8:00 a.m. for lab work, meeting with the doctor at 9 a.m. and beginning treatment at 9:30. Treatment would finish up at about 4:00 in the afternoon. Once I completed the first four treatments, the morning schedule would remain the same, but I would finish at about 2:00.

I would also need to give myself an injection the day after each treatment to boost my immune system. The Neulasta would help the body make more neutrophils, a type of white blood cell. I don't like needles, and I hate being sick, and knowing I needed to go to the clinic to undergo treatment that would make me feel worse was less than appealing. The reality that I would be losing my hair was also becoming more real the closer it got. I didn't want to be bald any more than I had wanted a bilateral mastectomy, but here we were. So I marched on, putting one foot in front of the other.

Prior to my initial chemotherapy appointment, I underwent a short surgical procedure to implant a chemo port beneath the skin on my chest. A port is a small, implanted reservoir with a thin tube that attaches to a vein. This device has the advantage of delivering chemotherapy medications into the port instead of a vein, which eliminates the need for needle sticks.

Before I went to the clinic for day one of chemo, I covered the port area with Lidocaine numbing cream and put plastic wrap over it. When I arrived at the clinic, they inserted the central line into my port. The Lidocaine ensured that I didn't feel any pain while they performed that task. So far, so good.

Next, I waited to see the oncologist. The nurse came in and took my vitals. My blood pressure was 152/94, much higher than my normal 120/68. She said, "Dr. Adebayo will be in soon, and then he will take you over to the chemotherapy area."

When the doctor came in, the first thing he said was, "Your blood pressure is high today. What's going on, Angela?"

Seriously?! My filter vacated my body, and I heard the sarcasm dripping from my voice. "Um, I don't know. I'm about to start chemotherapy???" He looked at me with a smile that I am sure he meant to be reassuring, but I saw only pity. "Let's walk you over to chemotherapy, shall we?"

The staff was kind. They put me in a room and offered me a heated blanket. As I settled in, I told the nurse about the blood pressure exchange. She laughed out loud and told me not to worry about the blood pressure. "It's not that uncommon. The first day of chemo can be stressful."

"Sorry to interrupt," said a young man carrying a menu. "My name is Dan, and I'm a volunteer. Some people just call me the snack guy." He winked at me. "Would you like something to eat or drink?"

"Can I get a Diet Pepsi?"

"Of course. And while I'm grabbing that soda"—he gestured to the table next to the bed—"take a look at that menu and circle what you would like for lunch. I'll be right back."

As I surveyed the menu, the nurse handed me another sheet of paper. "If there is anything we can get you at any time, just let us know." It surprised me to see a list of games, cards, puzzles, and reading material. Heck, I could even borrow an iPad if I wanted to. This was not what I had envisioned at all.

The nurse explained that first they would give me three different anti-nausea meds through my port. "You will also take two other anti-nausea meds home in case you need them, but those I'm giving you now should take care of the first forty-eight hours."

Dan returned with my Diet Pepsi. "Just in time," the nurse said. "Next, I'm hanging a bag of saline. We need to hydrate you before we start the chemotherapy medications. Before I do that, though, can I get your name and birthdate?"

"But then you'll know how old I am," I joked. "Angela Jeske. 3-3-65."

"Okay. Some people report a slight metallic taste with the saline, but if that happens, your soda should take care of it." She started the saline drip and almost immediately, I reached for my Diet Pepsi. I would not label this a "slight taste." It was the worst metallic taste I had ever experienced. It made the metallic flavor of the original Tab soda in the 1970s seem insignificant. I appreciated my soda, as it did mask the awful taste. My heart swelled with gratitude as the nurse handed me a heated blanket, providing solace from the icy sensation taking over my body from the inside out. This was the effect of the saline moving through my veins.

At about 10:00 a.m., the nurse came back into the room and told me it was time to begin the first chemotherapy drug. At that moment, I realized the metallic taste had vanished as quickly as it had appeared.

"This one is called Doxorubicin or Adriamycin," the nurse continued. For the third time today, she asked my name and birthdate. I was noticing a pattern; any time they were injecting me with something, they had to ask those two questions. It became a standing joke.

"What if my brain fog gets so bad that I don't know the answer?" I joked with the nurses.

I was grateful they made sure they were giving me the correct meds. It's bad enough to understand that they are injecting medications into your body to eradicate cancer, but it would be awful if they gave me someone else's "poison."

"We administer this medication a bit differently," said the nurse as she drew the bright red medication from the bag into a large syringe an inch in diameter and about 12 inches long. "I have to sit next to you and administer this medication slowly so that you only receive what your body can handle at one time." I will not lie; that seemed a little concerning.

Throughout this lengthy process, lasting more than an hour, I felt bad for the nurse, who had to be seated there the whole time. "Since we are hanging out," she joked, "I will tell you about the medication we are administering right now. The biggest shock to people is that when they go to the bathroom, this medication leaves the body looking pretty much like it looks going into the body, so your urine will appear to be bright red. Do not be concerned; you are not bleeding." Within ten minutes, I felt nauseous. The nurses had told me that sometimes hard candy helps with this, so I popped a Werther's Original caramel candy in my mouth and smiled in relief.

"This drug is also extremely toxic, so it is very important that after you use the bathroom, you carefully clean the area. Should anyone else come into contact with your urine, they need to wash their hands immediately with soap and hot water." It was at this moment that the reality of what they were pumping into my body hit me. Chemotherapy drugs are no joke. They are toxic—toxic to cancer cells, but also toxic to my body and, potentially, to my kids or anyone else who might use my bathroom.

Just as I was thinking we would never finish this medication, the nurse announced, "Finished with the Red Devil for today."

After pulling on new gloves and grabbing the next bag, she said, "This next drug is Cyclophosphamide. It is also known as Cytoxan or Taxol. We will administer this one the old-fashioned way. Can you tell me your name and birthdate?"

"I can, but I don't know if I should trust you with that information," I countered. Once I recited the requested information, she peeled my stickers off the sheet of paper and attached them to the bag of fluid.

The effects of the Cytoxan were apparent almost immediately, with fatigue and a clouded mind setting in. The nurse asked if I would like another heated blanket and I didn't hesitate before saying yes. If I had to list my favorite things about chemotherapy, heated blankets would top the list. No contest! Somehow, I always felt like a little girl wrapped in the comforting arms of a caring parent.

I dozed off for a while and when I woke up, Cade was there and so was my lunch.

"How was it?" he asked.

"Just your average day of being poisoned."

I didn't feel bad at all—a little foggy, but not sick. The day had passed quickly. I am not sure what I had been expecting, but the nurses had eased my fears and, in the end, the day was not bad. They told me that each treatment would affect me more than the one before, but I had already expected the worst and survived it. I wasn't ready to run a marathon, but I was feeling pretty good. And, just to be clear, there has never been a moment in my life when I was ready to run a marathon.

# Chapter 12

---

# Cancer May Change Your Perspective

"We must look at the lens through which we see the world, as well as the world we see, and that the lens itself shapes how we interpret the world."
Stephen R. Covey

C ompleting the first chemotherapy treatment brought gratitude. One down, only seven more to go. I enjoyed a peaceful evening following the first treatment, but it wasn't long after eating a small bowl of cereal that night that the first wave of nausea came. I took one of the nausea meds they had given me to take home, and I felt better within minutes. The next morning, I experienced another bout of nausea, but once again, one small miracle pill remedied it.

The picture in my head of cancer and chemotherapy prior to my experience was the pop-culture version. Every cancer movie I had ever seen reinforced my belief that chemotherapy would cause me to lose my ability to function and collapse on the bathroom floor next to the toilet. I thought of my grandmother and those of her generation who had to deal with the nausea and its consequences without the benefit of the medications. I had a lingering headache, but it was manageable. I felt a deep sense of appreciation.

The next hurdle was the Neulasta shot. I would need an injection the day following each chemotherapy treatment. Theoretically, I would take a preloaded syringe and stab it into my thigh. In reality, I couldn't make myself do it. I pulled back the plunger, checked to make sure there were no air bubbles, and poised my thumb to push the plunger once the needle was in my leg. Ready, aim ... My hand approached my leg, and just as the needle was about to connect with my skin, I pulled back. There was no way I could do this. I wasn't sure I could even watch Cade do it.

It was time for Plan B. Cade took the syringe and injected the back of my arm as I looked the other way. Damn, it burned, but it was done and the pain only lasted for a few seconds. Now, we were equipped with a plan for the day after chemo, and I did not need to poke myself with a needle. Small victories.

When we picked up the prescription the day before, the pharmacist said these little syringes cost $5,000 per shot. There is nothing I appreciate more than the fact that I am covered by good insurance, considering the expenses of $7,000 per chemo treatment, my surgical costs, and now the injections of Neulasta. At the end of my journey, which, fortunately, was less than a year long, my insurance paid over $300,000. It infuriates me when I think about how unfair it is that only privileged individuals have access to the highest quality healthcare.

Without adequate insurance, I might not have had the option to undergo the surgery, or maybe the recommendation would have been to have a lumpectomy instead of a mastectomy, resulting in the removal of only the three identified tumors with no knowledge of the additional eight lurking tumors, ready to proliferate. The option of a prophylactic bilateral mastectomy would not have been available to me, and I would have had to seek the funds for anything not considered "medically necessary" by a subpar insurance company. I was a single parent raising two children (still in my house) on a high school teacher's salary. I would not have been able to afford the best care.

The chemotherapy Dr. A referred to as my "insurance policy," would not have been available, potentially leading to the spread of cancer and leaving me with the choice of wearing a prosthesis or having an asymmetrical appearance because of the impossibility of paying for reconstruction. Luckily, this was not my reality.

This is why I've never made a big fuss about the fact that most years, I didn't receive a cost-of-living pay increase. Teachers give up those salary increases to keep what some call "Cadillac insurance plans." Are we underpaid for what we do? Yes, in my humble opinion, we are, but this is the tradeoff. Some of my teacher friends will never need such comprehensive insurance, but for those of us that do, it is more than worth it!

I was fortunate beyond just having great insurance, though. Most "good" insurance plans offer 80/20 coverage. The insurance company pays 80 percent and you pay 20 percent. Twenty percent of $300,000 is $60,000. I would not have been able to come up with $60,000 for the co-pay, in addition to paying my deductible, even if my insurance company had agreed to cover all my medical expenses.

I received my cancer diagnosis in 2011. I know I said that before, but it is important here. In March 2010, President Barack Obama signed into law the Affordable Care Act (ACA). This meant that my private insurance was required to cover women's preventative care, such as mammograms and cervical cancer screenings—with no cost sharing. It also meant that insurance companies were required to provide coverage for all cancer-related care. This meant that all of my surgeries associated with cancer, including reconstruction, were covered. Insurance covered chemotherapy and the Neulasta shot as well.

The point is that many of these things would not have been possible for me prior to 2010. I am not saying the Affordable Care Act is perfect; what I am saying is that it made it possible for me to get care that would have been unavailable to me, and until someone comes up with a better plan, I will argue with anyone who says this law has had a detrimental effect on Americans. I am still here, and I am cancer-free. For that, I'm grateful.

# Chapter 13

## What Others Think of Me Is None of My Business

"No one can make you feel inferior without your consent."
Eleanor Roosevelt

The two weeks that followed my first chemotherapy treatment were not terrible. By Sunday following my treatment, I had some fatigue and generally felt under the weather, but by Wednesday of the next week, I started to feel better, and in the second week I was pretty much back to normal. Now it was time for treatment number two.

This time my friend Jane came with me. The treatment went well, and it didn't affect me the way the first one had. I had less brain fog this time and none of the nausea I experienced before. I was able to chat with Jane and take a couple of brief naps with help from those amazing heated blankets.

I was struggling to maintain my composure, though. The morning of my second chemotherapy treatment, while taking a shower, I looked down to see a handful of hair. The sight of all that hair on the shower floor filled me with fear and sadness. I had no intention of reliving those emotions, or cleaning hair out of my shower every day. I had already talked to Cade and the kids because we knew this was coming. We had decided we would shave my hair down to a short buzz cut to minimize the hair mess all over the house as the rest fell out. I had no desire to be bald, but this was one of those situations where I had no choice, so I was determined to deal with it the best I could.

These where my thoughts as the nurse was finishing up the Doxorubicin and preparing the Cytoxan, complete with the required recitation of my name and birthdate. Noticing how quiet I was, Jane asked, "How are you doing, Angela?"

"Not bad for a woman who is going to make a production out of shaving her head tonight."

"You're losing your hair already?" Jane was my sponsor, and she guided me through my recovery journey. She was also my stand-in for Cade today.

"It started this morning, and I figure there's no reason to prolong the agony." I laughed because that's what I do. I laugh when I'm happy; I laugh when I'm uncomfortable; and sometimes I laugh when I'm miserable. Tears are for later when I'm by myself; they are not something I share with others.

"It's okay to be upset about losing your hair." Jane was a good sponsor. She was a kind, lovely woman in her eighties, but at that moment I wanted to slap her. It didn't matter how I felt; it was my reality and feelings wouldn't change that. Of course, that was my alcoholism speaking, suppressing my emotions rather than experiencing them. Jane was right, but that didn't mean I was ready to address how I felt right now. I said the "right" thing, hoping it would lead me to acceptance: "I know it's just hair. There are many people doing much worse than me." As if on cue, I heard the man in the room on the other side of my bathroom began another spasmodic coughing jag.

I was struggling, but I didn't want to cry. I was losing another piece of my identity. First my boobs and now my hair. Apparently, God had decided that I needed to address my character defect of vanity. As usual, I didn't like this plan, but if my program of recovery hadn't taught me that I couldn't control everything, my journey through cancer was determined to provide that lesson.

I have always had strong feelings about the societal perceptions of women and men. Hair loss is just one example. We see a bald man and we think ... Well, we actually think nothing. We don't stop and consider why he is bald; we don't think "that poor man"; we don't pause to think at all. But when we see a woman who is bald, whether she is wearing a scarf or a hat or just allowing us to see her bald head, we can't help but think about what the backstory might be. I knew this and had even taken part in it from the viewpoint of the observer. Now it had changed, though, because I was about to become the object. I prided myself on being a strong, independent woman and I did not want people to look at me the way they look at a cancer patient. I did not need anyone's pity. The idea of it pissed me off. I would get used to this, but I would never grow to like it.

On the way home from the clinic after treatment number two, I couldn't help but perseverate about chemotherapy. First, the doctor prescribes a poison. Then someone gets paid to inject that poison into your body. The purpose of said poison is to kill any remaining cancer. It does not know the difference between bad cells and good cells, so it kills some of the good cells too. And that boys and girls is why Cade and my kids gathered with me in the kitchen that night to shave my chin length layered bob into a buzz cut using the #2 guard on the electric clipper.

I wish I could remember more about the actual process of shaving my head, but this is one of the many gaps in my memory. I'm not sure if this is because of the chemo-induced brain fog or if it speaks to the trauma of this night for me. My kids have little specific recollection of this night, either. All of us remember a lot of laughter, which makes sense because it has always been how we deal with difficult emotions. Some might call it avoidance, but for us, it is just how we cope. We each need to deal with our feelings in our own time in our own way.

Maybe this is a throwback to the days when I drank to numb my feelings. When I quit drinking, I believed I had pretty much one emotion: anger. I didn't allow myself to experience the others. I'd made progress since then, but I still disliked experiencing my emotions and I certainly didn't want to experience them in front of others, even if those others were my children.

I sat in a chair in my kitchen with a towel around my neck and said, "Okay, here's to hoping I don't have a bumpy, lopsided head." We all laughed a little louder than necessary, especially me. It reminded me of all the self-deprecating jokes I used to make when I was drinking. I never thought they were particularly funny, but I prefer being the one cracking jokes at my own expense rather than being the target of jokes made by others. I had returned to my default setting.

I remember Cade shaving the sides first and leaving me with a Mohawk. Everyone laughed and insisted it was funny. I went to the bathroom to look, and as goofy as it looked, I remember experiencing this unsettling fear of the unknown. I wasn't really worried about what others would think; everyone expected me to lose my hair. And I was never one of those girls who spent hours in front of the mirror doing my hair and makeup. But now that I would not have hair, I seemed obsessed with the idea of my identity being wrapped up in it. Something else gnawed at me. Why should I still, at forty-six years old, be concerned with the loss of my hair and the opinions of others? I hated this!

I guess what bothered me most was my desire to be "normal." Why couldn't I be okay with just being me as I was at this moment? I have always found it challenging to feel like I belong. I never felt like I fit in, and I had been seeking the validation of others my whole life. Cancer was just a new twist on an old theme. This bald head would be a guarantee that I would not fit in. How could I with this shining globe atop my shoulders. At that moment, all I wanted was to be judged because I was having a bad hair day. I wanted to believe I was being stared at due to my bad haircut or not having time to wash my hair before school. Somehow, the looks of pity because I had cancer seemed worse than the whispers of judgment.

I returned to the kitchen and I'm sure we made jokes, but I don't remember any of them, and I doubt there is any reason I should remember them. What I remember is trying to focus on making this less difficult for my kids, which meant I needed to keep it together. I tried not to look at the hair hitting the floor, and Rae tried to sweep it up right away so that I didn't have to. At the end of the night, we hugged and took pictures and then, like so many other nights, I locked myself in the bathroom and cried.

I laid awake long after everyone else was sound asleep. Since my cancer diagnosis, for better or worse, this is when I did most of my mental processing. On this night, I thought about a piece of advice I had heard often around the tables of Alcoholics Anonymous. It goes something like this: "What other people think of me is none of my business." A lot of us have issues with ego and this quote is a quick reminder that others' opinions of us don't matter. I have spent a lot of wasted energy in my lifetime worrying about what others are thinking about me when the truth is they have a thousand more important things to think about. I am not the center of the universe and to spend my time stuck in my head obsessed with what others may or may not be saying about me is pretty damn egotistical. And even if they are talking about me, so what? If they are judging me, which is not likely, what am I going to do about it? I mean, do I really care what someone who is a crappy enough person to belittle someone with cancer thinks of me? And maybe they are talking about how they can help me and my family. That would be okay, because one of my other character defects is that I suck at asking for help.

Implementing this piece of advice is far more challenging than contemplating it, but it gave me a starting point. When it seemed to me people were staring or talking about me, I would just repeat this mantra to myself: "What other people think of me is none of my business."

For now, I still had a little hair, and I was determined to rock the buzz cut until the rest of my hair fell out. I mean, it would certainly take a lot less time to get ready to leave the house in the morning.

And thus began my Hat Era. I opted for this rather than wearing a wig for reasons that I am still unsure of. I think I was just determined that if I couldn't have my hair, I wouldn't have hair. That's me, stubborn and not always logical. I had collected a variety of hats over the past couple of months. It may seem odd, but one of the first things people do when they find out you're having chemotherapy is offer headwear.

Fashionista Friend: "I have some cute hats. I'll bring them over."

Friend with Lupus: "I have tons of hats. I will bring some of the ones I don't wear anymore when I visit." I thought this would be a few hats; it was a large Rubbermaid container.

Friend Whose Grandpa Died from Cancer: "We have some of grandpa's hats. You can have them." I was not optimistic about this one, but it turns out grandpa had some cool hats. Go grandpa!

In the end, I gained more hats than I could possibly wear in the few months that I would need them, but I appreciate those who reached out to offer help, and many of those hats became my staples for the next few months.

As time went on, I found myself increasingly capable of not focusing on what others thought about my appearance. I'm not sure if this was because I didn't care or if I was just too tired to care, but I can honestly say that over a decade later, I no longer spend time on what others think about me. Not often, anyway.

# Chapter 14

# True Friends Get You in All Your Brokenness

"Friends hold a mirror up to each other; through that mirror they can see each other in ways that would not otherwise be accessible to them, and it is this mirroring that helps them improve themselves as persons.

Aristotle

I woke up on Saturday, the day after the shaving of the locks, with a positive attitude considering I had just been infused with poison again. All things are relative when you're a chemotherapy patient, and relatively speaking, I didn't feel terrible. I was tired, though, so after Neulasta injection number two, I laid down to take a nap. When I woke up, I would decide what to do with my Saturday night.

That night, our local recovery club was having a karaoke night. I didn't feel much like partying, not even in the tame, sober sense of the word party, but my friends weren't having it. They were determined to get me out of my house because they suspected if I didn't get up and do something I would be having a private pity party. I had taken anti-nausea meds, and I was feeling rested, so I agreed, and Abbey and I headed for the club. I called Rae and invited her to come hang out with us. To my surprise, she convinced her brother and his girlfriend to come too. This was my first outing without a head full of hair and I was feeling pretty insecure, but it was nice to be doing something positive and fun with my kids.

I am no singer; I do not sing outside of my shower. My girls enjoy karaoke, though, and they were having a good time. I was still feeling a little crabby, but I had to laugh at what happened when my oldest daughter called her roommate to see if she wanted to join us. Now, my daughter and her roommate, Ashley were twenty-year-old Wisconsin girls, immersed in the alcohol culture that defines young Wisconsin twenty-somethings.

I heard Rae on the phone. "Hey, whatcha doing?"

Ashley: "Not much. Why?"

Rae: "You should come down to the Riteway Club."

Ashley: "Where's that?"

Rae: "It's on the north side. I'm here with mom. We are doing karaoke."

Ashley: "Rae, you know I don't have a fake [ID card]."

My daughter's machine-gun staccato laughter pierced through the music. Reigning in her laughter, she managed to say, "Ashley, it isn't that kind of club."

Ashley: "What?"

Rae: "It's alcohol free. It's the recovery club."

Ashley did join us and the girls all enjoyed themselves. Their laughter was loud, and their enthusiasm was a bit over the top, but I found them entertaining. They sang and they danced and you never would have guessed they were hanging out with a bunch of alcoholics in recovery.

On a break, Ashley sat down by me, looking more serious than she had all night. "I feel like everybody here thinks I'm drunk," she said.

Maybe she had a drink or two before she came out; I don't know. I do know my friends were not taking Ashley's inventory, though. It's not what we do in recovery. We work to keep our "own side of the street clean" and let others worry about their side of the street.

"Oh, honey, I promise you that none of these people are judging you. It's not what we do." As I mentioned in the previous chapter, I have found when I think others are worried about what I am doing (or how I look), it is usually because my ego is working overtime. I only *think* the rest of the world is obsessed with my thoughts and actions. I continued, "The truth is that everyone in this room has more important things to worry about. They are all trying to fix their own brokenness; I have found less judgment in this room than in any other room I have been in during my life."

I do not know if Ashley related to this, whether she retained this lesson, or if she even remembers the conversation, but this has been an important lesson in my life and the conversation that night was a good reminder that no matter what is going on in my life, I am not the center of the universe, whether I want to be or not. Sometimes during my cancer journey, I had a hard time understanding how others could not see that everything was about me. The stars had clearly aligned against me. What other explanation was there for everything I had been through in the past three months? I was an expert at throwing a good old-fashioned pity party. The truth was if I could just focus on others and their struggles, I would have less time to focus on mine. I learned that lesson at this club from some pretty awesome people.

I have had a lot of friends during different seasons of my life, and they all hold a special place in my heart, but none more than my friends in recovery. When I arrived in May 2009, I did not expect to make friends here. What I learned, though, is that these people "get me" in a way no one else ever has. They accept me as I am in all my brokenness. Never was this as true as it was during this year of my life.

I don't believe any of those sayings like "everything happens for a reason," and "God only gives you what you can handle." That's not how my God operates. However, I do think sometimes those of us who have had major struggles are uniquely equipped to help others later. God only reveals things to us when we are ready to hear them, though, and in January 2012 I was not ready to hear much of anything about how my journey through cancer might help others. I did know, however, that the people in this room had been to hell and back and they would not judge me for not being ready to let go of self-pity and focus instead on others. They would continue to hold me up and help me walk through the storm. And when the storm was over, they would help me pick up the pieces and move forward to give back to others. For that, I have an abundance of gratitude.

As the night wound to a close, I sat in a chair, feeling every bit of the fatigue that always descended on me a day and a half after chemo. I couldn't help but smile at my kids. It had turned out to be a good weekend, all things considered. The thing I had most been dreading, shaving my head, had left me and the girls laughing, even if there were tears for me later. And tonight, I was sitting in the club with my friends, watching my kids have fun. For these couple of hours, my cancer was not their focus. They seemed like they didn't have a care in the world and maybe they didn't for a couple of hours. And not one person said anything about my new hair or lack thereof. Thanks, friends.

# Chapter 15

# What We Say Matters

"Speak only if it improves upon the silence."
Mahatma Gandhi

Chemotherapy treatments continued through February, and they became increasingly difficult. The nausea turned into an ongoing battle, lasting for at least five days, and I no longer made any attempt to go back to school until the Wednesday following my treatment. It was frustrating to miss three days in a row when I would have much rather been in my classroom. Equally aggravating was the fog that enveloped me upon my return, as well as the increasing fatigue resulting from each treatment. I used to say I was so tired I could hardly move; now I knew what that really felt like.

I am so grateful for the patience of the people with whom I worked. I know I was not at the top of my game, but learning to accept myself at those times was all part of my learning curve. All I could do was my best and that seemed to operate on a sliding scale during the 2011– 2012 school year. Every day I woke up having no idea what my best would be that day, so I just put one foot in front of the other, recited the serenity prayer, and prayed for help getting through the day.

When I say I put one foot in front of the other, I mean that literally. My classroom was down a long hallway from the teacher's workroom. While other teachers often offered to do things for me to save me steps, I had to make the trek at least a couple times a day. The workroom was where I picked up my mail, made copies of things I had forgotten to take to the print shop, and ate my lunch. Walking was a slow, arduous process for me during the chemo months. My feet felt heavy, and I may as well have been trudging through a foot of mud. Progress was slow. I often stopped several times to rest and find the motivation to continue.

I will admit that at times my patience faltered—patience with the illness, with myself, and with others. Some days I thought, "How can people not hear how stupid they sound?" A good friend and I used to talk about this often. You do not say to a mother who has lost her child, "He's in a better place now" or "Everything happens for a reason." You don't tell those who are suffering, "It is all part of God's plan." And I have learned through experience that it is never a good idea to say, "It can't get any worse." Trust me, it can always be worse. Just say it, and you'll find out.

When I attended college at the University of Wisconsin–Eau Claire in the eighties, there was this footbridge I had to walk across to get from one class to another. Often when we met other students crossing the bridge, we would engage in what we called "bridge talk." It went like something like this:

"Hi. How are you?"

"Pretty good. You?"

"Same. See you later."

"Later."

This entire conversation took place without ever stopping or slowing our pace, and with no real thought given to what we were saying.

Flash forward to 2012. With schedules being what they were, I would meet the same people in the hall every day. One day as I was walking down that long high school hallway, I could see that I was about to meet one of those colleagues. I was feeling exceptionally tired, and I didn't want to talk to anyone, especially if it was going to be the same meaningless conversation I had repeatedly. On this particular day, I saw it coming and there was no way to avoid it, but my irritation had been building for weeks.

"Hi, Angela. How are you?"

"Not so great. I have cancer. How about you?"

I just kept walking, just as slowly as I had been before. I'm bald, pale, and shuffling down a hallway; how did it look like I was doing? I get it. It's polite to make conversation, but it is not necessary to ask questions that you already know the answer to. And asking a cancer patient how they are every single day? That seems like overkill to me.

I should probably feel bad about responding this way. I'm sure that this coworker was not trying to be unkind, but I didn't feel bad then and to be honest, I don't feel bad now. We need to think about the things we say to people, especially people who are struggling. It is our job as communicators and fellow human beings to practice empathy, and if we are not sure what to say to someone to be supportive and helpful, then the better choice is to say nothing.

# Chapter 16

# Prepare for the Unexpected

"The ultimate measure of a man is not where he stands in
moments of comfort and convenience, but where he stands at
times of challenge and controversy."
Martin Luther King, Jr.

B y the end of February, I had sores all over the inside of
my mouth. Eating was unbearable, and any acidic foods,
especially those that were tomato-based, were not an option.
The meals we received twice a week from the meal train were a
godsend, but this was when I realized how many common meals
have tomatoes or are tomato sauce–based. Fortunately, the nurses
gave me a recipe for a mouthwash that provided some relief, but
the mouth sores combined with the debilitating migraines and
fatigue left me wanting to curl up in a ball and stick my head under
my pillow.

I had no recollection of what "feeling good" entailed anymore.
There were days when I felt less awful, but good? Not even close.
Four months earlier, I didn't have a clue anything was medically
wrong with me. Now, it was hard to believe I would ever be healthy

again. I wanted there to be some reason I was going through this, but sometimes there are no answers. Cancer just sucks!

In March, we switched to the new chemo drug, and with that came a reprieve from some of the nausea and brain fog. Unfortunately, it also brought peripheral neuropathy pain in my hands and feet. Bruises appeared under my fingernails and toenails, and the pain in my hands and the bottoms of my feet was so intense that at times I couldn't bear weight, couldn't even hold a pencil.

I still taught seven out of every ten days in between treatments, and this took a toll on me. I was tired and I wished I could hide in a cave until I was on the other side of this. While it made sense that chemo caused my exhaustion, going to school every day and interacting with people all day long complicated matters.

I didn't know how I could keep teaching. I could barely make it out my door in the morning and I taught from my desk chair all day. That day, I called Human Resources to see if I had signed up for Short-Term Disability when I was hired seventeen years earlier. I was ready to explore whether taking some time off was feasible for me.

The sweet lady on the other end of the line said, "No. I'm sorry. You are not currently enrolled in Short-Term Disability. Is that a change you wanted me to make for you?"

I half-heartedly joked back, "I'm assuming it would not be retroactive?"

"I guess I'm not sure what you're asking."

"If I sign up for Short-Term Disability now, I would not be able to take time off to deal with my current cancer. Correct?"

I already knew the answer.

This was a difficult lesson. When they hired me, I was thirty years old. I had a five-year-old, a four-year-old, and a newborn baby. I wouldn't have said then that I felt invincible, but I could not foresee an instance in which I would need Short-Term Disability. In 1995, I was just trying to make ends meet and take care of my babies, and this seemed like one more unnecessary deduction from my paycheck. It was a small deduction every month and, looking back now, tears of regret pooled in my eyes.

When I was hired, I didn't even ask how much the deduction would be. To me, at the time, it was just another piece of paperwork I needed to complete.

At any point in my career, I could have gone back and changed this, but why would I? There were so many other priorities in my life, and I wasn't sick or injured. At this moment, I would have given anything for a time machine set to 1995. If I could have a conversation with my younger self, one thing I would tell her is that it is important to prepare for the unexpected because we never know what hardship may come our way. We are not invincible. Too many times in my life, I have found myself in the midst of a pity party asking, "Why me?" Here is a better question. "Why not me?" What makes me so special that bad things shouldn't happen to me, but should land on the doorstep of others?

I thought about this again several years ago when we were considering a change in insurance plans at my workplace. There was a lot of debate, during which I heard things like this:

"My whole family is healthy. We don't need all that coverage."

"We will never even pay our whole deductible. How does this help me?"

"Why should we be charged more due to the high medical expenses of others?"

Sometimes it is difficult to see things outside of our own life experience. In September 2011, when my school year began, I found myself in a state of good health. All my family members were also healthy. It would have been easy to assume that I had far more insurance coverage than I would ever use. In October, I had a routine annual mammogram and learned I wasn't as healthy as I thought. In November, I underwent a very costly bilateral mastectomy and from January through April 2012, I received treatment and underwent additional procedures. In September, I didn't know how badly I needed quality health insurance. Without that insurance, I would have either needed to find $300,000 that was not available to me or forego important medical care.

I am confident that there were years when my family did not exhaust our deductible, and it is possible that I was paying extra to ensure someone else had the necessary coverage. Had I considered that, maybe I would have been frustrated, but I like to think I am more empathetic than that. I like to believe I would have wanted that other person to be able to access the amazing medical care I had access to. I know I am blessed because I have been able to afford this insurance and because I chose a career with good benefits, and I also know not everyone is so fortunate.

Sometimes we genuinely cannot afford or otherwise obtain items or resources that may have future significance, but I have come to understand the importance of considering the potential and evaluating the expenses and possible consequences in case, by chance, the worst-case scenario occurs. I never cease to be grateful that I had good insurance and while I could not take additional time off work, it wasn't the end of the world. Working contributed to my exhaustion, but it also gave me a distraction and kept me from burying myself under my negative emotions. When I left that employer and took a different teaching job, though, you better believe I signed up for Short-Term Disability.

# Chapter 17

# Everything Is Easier When You Laugh

"Power, money, persuasion, supplication, persecution—these can lift at a colossal humbug—push it a little—weaken it a little, century by century, but only laughter can blow it to rags and atoms at a blast. Against the assault of laughter nothing can stand."
Mark Twain

I n the chemotherapy unit, the nurses bring you pretty much anything you want. For me, this was usually a Diet Pepsi and a snack. My favorite nurse, Debbie, liked to say, "It's so easy to keep you happy."

I always brought a friend with me so I would have someone to chat with until Cade got there. Sometimes we would try to watch a show, or I might try to grade some papers. That was never a very successful endeavor due to my brain fog and distractibility. I always asked for a heated blanket as soon as I got settled in and every time it cooled off, I would ask for a replacement. At some point in the day, this usually led to a nice nap.

I no longer had high blood pressure when I arrived at the clinic, and I no longer felt like my heart would explode from my chest when the nurses hooked me up to the chemo. I had grown used to the fact that poison was pumping through my veins, and I accepted that this was the best way to prevent my premature exit from this world. I no longer needed to remind myself that there are people with worse problems than me; I knew it was true.

There were eighteen chemotherapy beds in the cancer unit, and they seemed to be consistently full. I had seen elderly patients, and I had seen patients decades younger than me. It was generally pretty quiet other than the customary sounds of wheels as they moved IV carts from room to room and the beeping of calls to the nurse's station.

One Friday, I woke from a nap and since my blanket had cooled off, I made my way to the bathroom. I managed to extricate myself from the blanket and then rose to my feet, double-checking that all the tubes fastening me to the IV pole were untangled. I'm not the most coordinated person, and I could envision myself tripping and falling on my face. I wheeled the pole to the bathroom adjoining my room to my neighbor's room and locked the door so that I wouldn't have a surprise visitor. A nurse in the next room was talking to the room's occupant, who, based on the volume with which she was speaking to him, was an older gentleman.I

t took me a few minutes when I returned to my bed to get situated again and I had just settled in when I heard my neighbor yell, "I forgot something!" I'm not sure why he didn't use his call button, but his volume caught my attention. "Could you bring me a beer chip?"

I stopped and looked at my friend, puzzled. She looked confused; I assumed for the same reason I was. I know they will bring you pretty much anything you want here, but a beer chip?

I'm not sure if they have these everywhere, but in Wisconsin beer chips are a thing. Sometimes at a bar, one customer wants to buy another customer a drink and instead of sending an actual drink, the bartender gives them a chip that says, "One free drink." That way, they can turn in the chip for a drink of their choice when they are ready.

Not much surprised me anymore, but I must admit this encounter left me with questions. First, why would he be asking for a beer chip? And second, did they really hand out beer chips at chemo?!

It turns out I didn't have to wait long to find out. The nurse came back down the hall and as she entered his room, I heard her ask in a voice reserved for conversations with those who are hard of hearing, "What do you need a Q-tip for?"

I started giggling, and I could not stop. My friend looked at me, more confused than before, and finally she asked, "Did I miss something?"

I told her what I thought he said, and we both started laughing. Most people wouldn't have found this so funny, and maybe you're thinking, This woman had clearly lost her mind. To two women in recovery, though, it was good for a laugh. Clearly, I have the brain of an alcoholic, even when I'm sober.

Through my tears I finally managed to say, "Of course I would hear beer chip."

With a sigh, I pushed my call button to ask for another heated blanket. And of course, I told the nurse the story. I mean, why wouldn't I? She was a captive audience, after all. I don't know if she thought it was that funny, but she was a good sport, so she played along.

I had become used to chemotherapy and it no longer gave me the anxiety it had at the beginning, but to say it was pleasant would be a stretch. The nurses were amazing and no amount of appreciation for what they do every day would be enough. They kept me comfortable and brought me whatever I wanted. So I had adjusted to the process, but to say I had no anxiety would not be accurate. Every time I was hooked up to the chemo drugs, I knew that what was flowing through my veins was poison designed to kill any cancer cells in my body, and because the drugs flowed through my whole body, in the process they would damage healthy cells as well. This is why my hair fell out and it was why I would experience nausea and increased fatigue in the next couple days. Because of my propensity for overthinking things, this meant chemo would always be an emotional challenge for me.

Moments like these helped, when I found something to laugh about, no matter how silly. Laughter continued to be my best medicine. I wasn't laughing at the man in the next room. I didn't know him. I had no idea what kind of cancer he had or how sick he was. I was laughing at myself, at the fact that what I heard was because of my own "less than perfect" past. In the end, it didn't matter what I laughed at. As long as I continued to find things that sparked my sense of humor, I believed I would be okay. The hard things in my life have always been just a little easier when I can laugh about them.

# Chapter 18

# We Can't Control the Outcome

"If things do not turn out as we wish, we should wish for them
as they turn out."
Aristotle

I sat in front of my computer googling "fingernails and chemotherapy," certain that the giant cancer binder the oncology nurses had given me did not mention what I was seeing as I looked at my hands. I had noticed some discoloration on my nails about a week before. It looked a bit like bruising and I didn't think too much about it at first, but my fingers continued to hurt and the discoloration was now brown and green and less than attractive. When I was first diagnosed and they gave me the resource binder, I sat down and read straight through the entire binder. This is how I knew there was nothing in there about fingernails, so this time I went to Dr. Google. When I saw the list of potential issues on various medical sites, I was a little freaked out:

- Changes in nail color

- Changes in nail shape or texture, such as grooves or ridges

- Nail separation from the skin below

- Pain around the fingernails or toenails

Why had I not seen any of this in my binder? I read further that the changes in nails may make it difficult to do things like picking up a pencil or buttoning jeans, and that some people found it difficult to walk. Now I was becoming frustrated. This had to be what I was experiencing. I hadn't connected the pain in my hands and my feet to the discoloration in my fingernails until I read this, but here it was in print.

My fingers ached, and I tried to stretch them several times a day. Buttoning my jeans was challenging, but that is why they make elastic waist dress pants and skirts, right? It brought me a sense of relief knowing that I could still hold a pen. Given the struggles I was already facing in performing my job, I didn't need any additional complications from the cancer gods. My foot pain was significant enough that I planned the shortest route between points A and B and asked the kids to bring me things so that I didn't have to put weight on my feet. Sometimes, I still had intense stabbing pain in my feet when I was just sitting in my chair. It felt like someone was simultaneously stabbing needles into my feet and setting them on fire. Those pains came randomly and there were times when I actually cried out because they were so unexpected.

When I first stood up to walk, it was the worst. I couldn't have hurt more if I had run a marathon while wearing three-inch stilettos. I thought the balls of my feet were surely bruised, but when I looked at my feet, they appeared perfectly normal. I soaked my feet in Epsom salts, I put lotion on them, and I tried to massage them, but touching them at all caused an increase in pain. And nothing seemed to make them feel better.

These were the conditions I was operating under as I gingerly approached the registration desk for chemotherapy treatment number seven.

The receptionist, Roxanne, said, "Hi. Angela. How are you today?"

"Oh, I'm good." Yes, I was lying, but this is the Midwest and there is only one appropriate response when someone asks how you are.

"I need your birthdate, hon." We may be on a first name basis, but this was, after all, protocol, and I no longer even took the time to joke about it.

I rattled off my birthdate, and she said, "Okay. It should just be a minute."

I was moving so slowly that I hadn't even sat down in the waiting room when the nurse came to get me. She looked at me quizzically and asked, "Are your feet bothering you?"

"They are awful. Sometimes I can hardly walk at all."

She said, "That's from the chemo. You should talk to Dr. Adebayo about it when you get back there." I knew better than to hope there would be a solution, but I hoped he could at least tell me how long this would last.

I was determined to not be annoyed when he came in today. For some reason, his overly upbeat demeanor always seemed to annoy me. I don't know why, but unlike the chemo nurses, he seemed less than genuine to me. He smiled a little too big and his enthusiasm was constant. Sometimes I thought a little more empathy and a little less perky cheerleader would have been nice.

He entered with that same ostentatious smile. "How is Angela today?"

"She's been better." Yup. That was a snarky English teacher's response, but my feet hurt and responding in kind to a conversation about myself in third person was pretty much the nicest thing I could come up with at the moment.

"What's going on?"

I detailed what was going on with my fingers and my feet.

"Ah. That's the chemo. It's to be expected."

"Of course it is," I responded sarcastically. "Everything is from the chemo." I instantly felt sorry for being a bitch, but it was about to get worse.

I held up my hands to show him my fingernails and said, "Is this lovely camouflage fingernail thing part of that too?"

"Yes. That usually happens before your fingernails fall off."

"What?! Why didn't I know my fingernails were going to fall off? I swear you didn't tell me that."

"It doesn't happen for everyone, but it is common."

How could he not have told me that this was a likely outcome? He was so quick to tell me that my hair would fall out and when that would happen that it never occurred to me there were things I wasn't being told. This felt so disrespectful to me. I am an intelligent, educated woman. Why would this doctor, an oncology specialist, not give me all the information so that I could process it? I know that having this information wouldn't have changed the outcome. There was nothing I could have done with the information to keep my fingernails and toenails from falling off, but I couldn't help feeling like I had a right to know. I felt betrayed, and that sentiment had my righteous indignation and judgmental attitude flaring.

Often in my life, my feelings have been bruised because of the expectations I hold for others. In this case, my expectations were irrational. I had expected this doctor to give me all the possible outcomes. I thought he should understand that I needed all the information I could get because it was important to me to feel in control, even though that control would just be an illusion. This was my deep-seated belief that I could control outcomes.

In recovery, I have learned that I cannot control how things will turn out; "all I can control is myself and how I respond." I must let my Higher Power take care of the outcome. I don't know why Dr. Adebayo didn't tell me that losing my fingernails and toenails was a possibility. Maybe he thought there was no point in telling me about things that might not happen, and maybe that would have been the best decision for another patient. I don't know. I'm an alcoholic and I will always think like an alcoholic to some degree. This alcoholic tends to think, even today, that I can control the outcomes in my life.

Here is what I have learned, though. Being sober gives me a freedom to live my life that I didn't have when I was drinking, and that freedom allows me to make decisions. Sometimes the choices I make influence the outcome, and sometimes they don't. There is nothing I could have done, in this case, that would have impacted the outcome. No matter what I did my nails still would have fallen off and I still would have been upset about it. Was I angry with my doctor or was I angry with cancer?

I stared at Dr. A incredulously.

He went on to explain. "Chemotherapy kills cancer cells, but it doesn't know the difference between bad cells and good ones. That is why your hair falls out and it is also why you can lose fingernails and toenails, but it is not the same for everyone."

This made sense to me, and I nodded in defeat. Cancer wins again.

"Do you have other questions for me?" he asked.

"Yes. How long is this pain in my hands and feet likely to last?"

"For some people, it passes quickly. For others, it may last for a month or two past the end of your chemotherapy. In some cases, the pain may pass, and you may have some numbness for several months."

"Okay. Thank you for the information." I could feel my bad mood starting to pass, as I wished the pain in my hands and feet would. I asked hesitantly, now feeling the shame that followed my outburst, "Is there any chance I could get a handicapped parking pass to limit how far I have to walk?"

"Of course." And just like that, he handed me the parking pass paperwork, and I walked haltingly to chemotherapy, looking at the floor and wincing with each step.

I wasn't mad at Dr. Adebayo; I was angry with cancer. I was angry and I was tired. I was so very tired – physically and emotion-ally. Cancer changes so much. Some of it is temporary and some of it is permanent. The hard thing is that we never really know how long the battles will be or how steep the mountain of adversity. At this point in my journey, I was literally just putting one foot in front of the other. Later, I would need to learn to adjust to my "new normal". Today, I understand that even as a cancer survivor, I will never be the same person I was before my diagnosis. I haven't always liked that, but I have come to accept it.

# Chapter 19

# Fake It Till You Make It!

*"Fake it until you make it! Act as if you had all the confidence
you require until it becomes your reality."*
Brian Tracy

"Fake it till you make it." I heard this phrase often from
other alcoholics in recovery, but I never truly understood
it until my little jaunt through chemotherapy. It was this phrase
that popped into my head as I made my way to the chemo wing,
looking at my discolored fingernails.

"Hi, Angela. Get comfortable and put in your order for lunch
while I get everything ready to go." I always felt welcomed here;
the chemo nurses were amazing and Debbie was my favorite.

I settled in, ordered my Diet Pepsi to mask the metallic taste of
the saline, as well as my sandwich for lunch; the sandwich would
probably would go home with me and become my supper."

Alrighty, hon. Name and birthdate?"

"This is so much easier than it used to be," I joked, as I echoed
the same information I would repeat three more times before I
left for home later in the day.

Debbie hooked me up to the saline and sat down to chat. "You
didn't bring anyone for company today?"

"Nah. I'm an old pro now. I don't need the same moral support as I used to. Maybe I will just catch a nap later. It's a lot easier when no one is staring at me, feeling like they should make conversation."

"A nap is always a good plan. Maybe I'll kick back in the recliner over there and take one with you."

"Sounds like a plan to me. Just make sure to grab one of those heated blankets; they are better than Ambien." I grinned at her, feeling better than I had felt in days.

These nurses were amazing. It felt like I had known them forever. When I was nervous, they put me at ease and when I was melancholy, they lifted my spirits. I don't know what the salary is for a chemo nurse, but whatever it is, it is not enough. Often, I thought about how difficult this job must be. One patient uses chemo as a prophylactic measure hoping to prevent future cancer; another simply hopes to survive long enough to witness the birth of their grandchild or the marriage of their daughter; still another decides this will be their last round of chemo. I honestly don't think I could do it. It takes a special person to go to work every day where people are dying and still be so upbeat and kind.

"So, how have the last couple of weeks been?"

"Just amazing." I held my hands up, wiggling my fingers. "Aren't they beautiful?"

"That looks like some painful bruising."

"This? I'm thinking I can market it."

I launched into my best announcer voice, born from years of teaching high school speech classes. "Ladies and gentlemen. Check this out. Are you going through chemotherapy? Or maybe you miss your chemo days. We have you covered. Our chemo camo nail polish sells for just $9.99. Such a bargain compared to actual chemotherapy. No nausea. No fatigue. Just beautiful camouflage nails."

A genuine smile lit up Debbie's face. "I love your sense of humor, Angela."

"I'm seeing ad campaigns and maybe a national tour. Oprah could interview me. I can see it now. The whole audience goes home with a sample. Pointing, I say, 'Camo Chemo Polish for you and for you and for you.'"

"Heck, I could be a hand model," I continued. "I hear they sometimes make upwards of $1,000 a day. I could buy a lot of nail polish for that. What a deal! Much better than actual chemotherapy."

I joined Debbie in unbridled laughter, the kind that requires your entire body. As the laughter subsided, she said, "Seriously, Angela. I think you are my most optimistic patient. You have such a positive attitude, and that attitude plays as big a part in your recovery as the chemotherapy."

"I bet you say that to all the Chemo Queens," I bantered as I adjusted my invisible crown.

"You never let things get you down. Losing fingernails can be difficult, and yet here you are making fun of cancer and chemotherapy. I wish all my patients could do that. It is such a gift."

I could have told her it was all a cover, my shield, to keep the world from seeing how vulnerable I felt, but I didn't. I realized as I left that day that I had been "acting as if." As if I didn't care if I lost my nails. As if it was no big deal. As if it wasn't making me feel ugly and defeated and hopeless. The shield of "acting as if" had worked, if only for a short time. For those couple of hours in the chemo unit, I had power over my sadness. I felt like the old Angela, the one who could make jokes and laugh at the things that threw me off balance. This sadness would return intermittently, but I knew it couldn't defeat me.

I was beginning to see a pattern emerge. I could walk through tough stuff—surgery and the pain following it; chemo and all the illness and fatigue that transpired. What punched me in the gut, though, were the losses. I had lost my breasts, then my hair, and now my fingernails and toenails. I would have the breast reconstruction, and my hair and nails would grow back, but at the moment, that knowledge was not helping my mood. Recovery and cancer were conspiring to teach me that logic and emotions are not always good playmates. My sponsor once told me that it was all right to "act as if" I was strong, until I actually felt that strength. I would need to address this lack and learn to access tools other than self-deprecating humor, but for now I just needed to plod on. Therapy would come later.

# Chapter 20

---

# Choose Your Battles

"Action is a great restorer and builder of confidence. Inaction
is not only the result, but the cause of fear."
Norman Vincent Peale

I f you have ever visited the Department of Motor Vehicles
(DMV), you probably left with at least one complaint. At least
that's been my experience in Wisconsin. Prior to 2012, I had two
chief complaints: wait time and lack of customer service.

I have visited the DMV many times since I turned sixteen. It
always seems to look the same. Check in; show them your driver's
license. They give you a ticket with a number on it, and you wait.
There are screens with numbers flashing all over the room, but
there seems to be no actual organization to the numbers flashing
on those screens. This is frustrating for those of us who like order. I
just want to know when I can run to the bathroom without missing
my number and being banished to the end of the invisible line.

As I waited, I would play this game where I tried to figure out
which one of the DMV employees looked most like they might
crack a smile or at least be more friendly than Attila the Hun. I
always felt like a student waiting to speak to the principal.

It is fair to say my trips to the DMV are among my least favorites.
They rank up there with the dentist's office for me. It was March

2012, though, which meant I needed to renew my driver's license. These were the conditions under which I walked into the DMV that March, wearing my hat to cover my bald head and dreading, as usual, the entire experience.

I collected my ticket and settled in to wait. When my number appeared on the screen, I went to the window, provided my paperwork, and showed my license again. They sent me to have my photo taken. Perhaps I should have added this to my list of complaints about the DMV. They are not known for their photography skills. It had never bothered me much, though. I mean, how often do you need to show anyone your driver's license?

Later that night, lost in my thoughts and depression following this trip to the DMV, I could better answer that question. You need to show your driver's license when you get stopped by a police officer; every time you fly; to purchase adult beverages, cigarettes, or other age-sensitive products; to sign up for services like a library card; and at least twice every time you go to the DMV. This list was generated as I replayed in my head the following scene.

The middle-aged man who called me to have my photo taken looked like he would rather be anywhere else. He was sporting a receding hairline and what we call a "beer belly" in Wisconsin. He didn't smile when he plucked me off the assembly line. I sat on the stool that was positioned in just the correct spot to get the less than perfect photo. This was the photo that once they placed it on the fire-engine red background would make even those who were model beautiful look like they had been ill with the flu for weeks.

I could not think of a worse time to need a photo. My skin tone had a dull pallor attributed to six chemotherapy treatments and even my hat didn't conceal the fact that I was clearly bald. I was determined to make the best of it, though.

"I need you to take the hat off."

"What?"

"I need you to take the hat off. No hats for the photos." He sounded like he was reading from a cue card.

Since when? I thought. I used to work in retail. I have seen many driver's licenses with men sporting baseball caps. Now all of a sudden, the female cancer patient has to take her hat off?

I decided to try humor rather than outrage. "I promise the hat is not concealing my hair color. I am bald as a cue ball from chemotherapy." I smiled.

"Ma'am, I'm just following the rules," he said in the same droning monotone.

"Well, can you explain the rules to me? The hair color I put on my license renewal application will not match the bald head in my photo anyway, so why do I need to take my hat off? I promise you it was not my choice to be bald and you are not helping right now."

"I can take the picture or not take the picture, but I can only take the picture if you remove the hat." Clearly this was going to be adversarial, and I doubted I would win this argument. I wasn't prepared to deal with this today.

My eyes brimmed with tears. "So, I have no choice?" I questioned as I blinked back the tears.

"Well, we can take the picture today or you can come back after your hair grows back and we can take the picture then," he offered, less than empathetically.

"But if I do that, my driver's license will expire."

He just shrugged his shoulders and stood, waiting. I didn't know this man, but at this moment, the animosity I felt toward him bordered on hatred.

"Is there anything to prevent me from coming in to get a new driver's license in six months?" I growled at him through my clenched teeth.

"Of course not, but there will be a nine-dollar fee."

Of course there will be. "Fine." Frustrated, I yanked the hat off my head and tossed it on the ground. "Let's get this over with."

"I will take the picture on the count of three," he recited. "Smile."

Like hell I would. One … Two … Click. A few minutes later I had a driver's license in my possession. I had the largest, baldest head I had ever seen, and my expression was one of complete dejection. Would it kill the Department of Motor Vehicles to get some filters for their driver's license pictures? I can go on Snapchat and put a turkey on my head at Thanksgiving time, for crying out loud. Why not a nice little hat that meets their specifications?

What kind of monsters do they hire at the DMV? What could be so miserable in this man's life that he decided to torture a cancer patient that day? All I knew as I made the walk to my car was that as soon as my hair grew back, I would fight the trauma response I was bound to have after today, walk back in, and replace this driver's license. Tears welled up again, and as I plopped onto the seat of my car, they were streaming down my cheeks. They could have been tears of embarrassment, but it is much more likely they were tears born of anger.

Unfortunately, this would not be the only trip I needed to make to the DMV during this battle. A couple weeks later, having procured the paperwork for a handicap-accessible parking permit from my doctor, I again ventured inside those ominous doors. I was moving more haltingly this time because of the pain in my feet. I made my way to the registration desk where the woman there gazed at me with an expression that I didn't quite understand at first. In a tone three shades too somber, she asked, "How are you today?" At that moment, I recognized the look on her face as unmitigated pity.

I knew I didn't look great, but this seemed like overkill. "I'm okay," I offered. "I just need to get a handicap parking permit. Here is the paperwork from my doctor." She took the paperwork and handed me the temporary permit. She explained it would expire in six months and, as though she thought the permit might outlast me, she lamented, "I hope you have some better days."

Sometimes during this journey, I laughed and sometimes I cried. This second trip to the DMV was so ridiculous that it made me laugh. I'm sure I looked like I was in significant pain, but I certainly wasn't wasting away, and I don't believe I looked like I was going to drop dead on the spot. This is a great lesson for all of us.

When we don't know the complete story, we should not respond as though we do. Her comment to me was way over-the-top. She could have simply said, "I hope your day gets better." That slight change in the sentence would make it more acceptable and less offensive. I repeated this story often, maybe because it was that funny or maybe because I hoped people would tell me I didn't look that bad.

Perhaps I could find humor in this story because, despite feeling offended, I recognized that this woman was attempting to display compassion towards me. I appreciated that perhaps more than I normally would because it was the opposite of what I experienced during my previous trip to the DMV.

The two visits that spring to the DMV gave me a little perspective. There are many things in my life that I complain about; trips to the dentist and to the DMV are just two of them. The reality is that those trips had just been an inconvenience. They had activated my impatience, and I had found them annoying. While I sometimes became upset on those trips, there had been nothing exceptionally upsetting about the visits. In contrast, these two trips differed from anything I had experienced previously at the DMV. Both experiences were traumatizing in different ways.

Today, when I find myself upset, I try to ask a couple questions. First, why am I upset? Second, is there anything I can do about it? If there is nothing I can do about it, then I take the steps to move on. When I was having my picture taken, I could have asked to speak to someone else. I could have just left and let my license expire. Instead, I decided to engage in a battle I would not win. During the second visit, instead of getting lost in feeling bad about myself, I could have confronted the DMV worker's ignorance. I could have politely informed her that I was almost done with chemo and I was cancer-free, suggesting that there was a good chance I would outlive her. I chose instead to let these events traumatize me. I was not in a safe space to deal with either a complete disregard for my feelings or the pity of others. That day would come, but it wasn't here yet.

# Chapter 21

# There's No Shame in Accepting Help

"Vulnerability is not winning or losing; it's having the courage
to show up"
Brené Brown

I was born in the sixties and, as with a lot of girls of that era, my upbringing instilled in me the values of being a strong and independent woman. Most of my friends throughout my four decades on the planet would have described me as just that, but I always felt like an imposter, and I spent a tremendous amount of time afraid others would discover I wasn't strong after all. The truth was that I couldn't let myself accept help from others because they might realize that this had more to do with my low self-esteem than with true strength. This is one of many things that led me to drink.

I had heard women in meetings talk about reaching out to others, but I still didn't know how to do that. In my early meetings, I was told to collect phone numbers from other women in the program. If I was feeling like drinking or even if I was feeling lonely, upset, angry, or any of the many other feelings that had often led me to drink, I was supposed to call one of those numbers and talk to someone. It wasn't even necessary to talk about what was bothering me; sometimes just having a conversation with another living, breathing individual would allow the feeling to pass.

At the time of my cancer diagnosis, I had been sober for two and a half years and I had called no one on that list. Even the idea of calling people and asking them for help caused an increase in my anxiety. I was overcome with a sense of vulnerability, convinced opening up would leave me susceptible to being hurt. Cancer has a way of calling bullshit, though.

I can't count the number of times after my diagnosis that someone said, "Let us know what we can do for you and the kids." I kept thinking, You're assuming I know what that is. Fortunately, I was surrounded by people who knew I was not likely to reach out. This was a blessing because they didn't wait; they just offered, and I learned to accept the help that was offered.

The first help we received originated at my workplace. As soon as I told them about my diagnosis, they set up a meal train. If you've never heard of this amazing creation, this is how it works. The organizer puts together a document with dates on it and people can sign up to make a meal for one or more of the dates. Because of modern technology, this requires minimal work by the organizer. They just create the form and then link it to social media accounts and send it out via email. People I worked with, people in my recovery groups, and other friends all signed up to make meals for us, resulting in a tremendous show of support. Even the kids in my school's National Honor Society participated.

The meals were helpful, and I loved to see the people who dropped them off. As a high school teacher, I especially enjoyed the visits from students. For weeks, the NHS kids delivered two meals a week. It was always a different group of three or four students. We would chat for a couple minutes, and they would be on their way.

One afternoon, a group of students brought a meal, and we chatted as usual. Before they left, one girl asked, "Could we get you to sign our community service form?" One requirement of

the National Honor Society is that students need to document
their community service hours. I smiled and signed their forms.
After they left, I chuckled to myself. This was the first group that
had asked me to sign their form. The others had been having the
guidance counselor or their advisor sign for them, and although
I knew how the community service component worked, it had
never entered my mind that while I'm sure these students wanted
to help me, they were also doing this for community service hours.
Most of the students understood it was more socially appropriate
to have their advisor sign the form than to ask for a signature from
the person they were delivering the food to. I wasn't upset. It made
me happy to see teenagers being teenagers. To these kids, I was
just Mrs. Jeske, their English teacher. I was craving just a bit of
normalcy in my life, and I could count on teens to provide it.

The second group that reached out to help me was my friends
in Alcoholics Anonymous. Yes, the same friends who I had never
called on outside a meeting. They didn't let that deter them,
though. They were there as soon as I first talked about my diagnosis at a meeting.

I have no idea how I would have gotten through this year in my
life if not for these women. After I found out I would need to have a
bilateral mastectomy and my recovery period would be six weeks,
I was terrified at the prospect of not being able to get to meetings.
This was my support system not just for how not to drink, but also
for how to deal with life. I couldn't imagine not being able to attend
meetings at all for the first few weeks after surgery. I was struggling
with this reality when a good friend told me the women would like
to bring a couple of meetings to my house if I was okay with that.
Okay with it? I felt like someone had thrown me a life jacket. It
wouldn't save me, but it just might help me keep my head above
water until I could get myself to shore.

The night of the first meeting at my house, my daughter went
downstairs to give us privacy. I longed to be a wonderful hostess,
but my strength faded, leaving me barely able to stand. These
ladies put me in a chair and came to me to visit prior to the

meeting. Then we arranged ourselves in a circle and the meeting began. This was a topic meeting. In a topic meeting, someone chooses a topic and then we all share something related to that topic. My friend and sponsee chose Acceptance as the topic. I couldn't imagine a better, or more difficult, topic for me right then.

She opened by sharing a passage that discussed the importance of acceptance in dealing with our problems, no matter what they are. The fundamental concept assumes that if something disturbs us, it is because we deem it unsatisfactory to our own standards and we need to accept it as part of life. Cancer and a bilateral mastectomy were more than unacceptable to me. The words "offensive" and "repugnant" came to mind. As Jamie read the passage, I realized I needed to accept that everything happens as it is supposed to and to experience any serenity, I would need to acknowledge that instead of continuing to fight it. I knew this reading. I had read it many times before—by myself, with sponsors and sponsees, and in meetings. It had never seemed as true as it did this time, though. Boy, did I find my present situation unacceptable. And I could not remember the last time I had experienced anything close to serenity.

As Jamie shared her thoughts, I heard this: If I wanted to feel better, I needed to focus on what needed to be changed in my attitude because there was nothing I could do to change the situation. I had started to believe that everything in my life had to happen as it did to lead me to sobriety, but how could I apply that to cancer? For the life of me, I couldn't imagine at that moment how changing something in me or my attitude would make me happy. Not as long as I was dealing with cancer.

I listened as others shared their experience, strength, and hope, and I reminded myself that this works. If it didn't, I wouldn't still be sober. Maybe I would hear something tonight that would resonate with me immediately or maybe it would have to percolate around in my brain for a while before I would be ready to use it, but I knew there would be something I needed to hear in this meeting. That is how it always worked. So I listened. And then I shared. Well, mostly I cried and expressed my gratitude. I do not know what I said, but I gained a lot of wisdom from others that night. And as I shared, I saw others wiping away tears too. It was an emotional meeting.

I wasn't ready yet, but during the next weeks and months, I started to look within myself for the solution. There was nothing I could do about the fact that I had cancer, so what could I change in me? I was spending far too much time feeling sorry for myself. I knew that, and if there was one thing I had learned in recovery, it was that our attitude has power. I could choose to be miserable, or I could choose to do something about it.

It made me think about a story I had heard. This story is generally attributed to the Cherokee or Lenape people. It starts with the premise that we each have two wolves inside of us. One is evil. It is anger, envy, sorrow, regret, greed, arrogance, self-pity, guilt, resentment, inferiority, lies, false pride, superiority, and ego. The other wolf is good. It is joy, peace, love, hope, serenity, humility, kindness, benevolence, empathy, generosity, truth, compassion, and faith. The story ends by asking: Which one will you feed?

I knew I did not want to feed the evil wolf. That is where I had lived when I was drinking, and I did not want to live there again. If I wanted the traits of the good wolf, I had to do the work. I started to focus on my faith and seeing the good in my world, even with cancer. I will admit this was a full-time struggle, and it took a long time for things to get better, but I was committed to feeding the good wolf, and it all started with those amazing women bringing the first meeting to my house.

A couple weeks later, they brought a second meeting to my house, chocolate themed this time. Yup, that is exactly what it sounds like. We had a traditional meeting and then we ate a variety of chocolate treats and visited. I've heard it said chocolate heals the soul. I would have agreed that night. Those ladies and that chocolate lifted my spirits in a way that nothing else had. I felt loved and cared for, and for maybe the first time in my life, I felt like I was a part of something bigger than myself.

These ladies continued to be there for me. After that second meeting, they drove me to meetings until I could drive again; we scheduled coffee dates and lunch dates; and I started to use that phone list to reach out when I was struggling. That passage on acceptance has guided my life in a way no other piece of writing has, and I have these women to thank for that. I do not know how I would have made it to the end of this journey without them.

My neighbors also reached out to me. Let me share a little bit about my neighborhood. This was a brand-new subdivision in 1998 when we moved into our house and, as often happens with new subdivisions, a lot of new families with kids bought houses there. My kids were two, three, seven, and eight when we joined the neighborhood. Most of us had kids about the same age and so we spent a lot of time outside with them in the summer. The kids would play and the adults would stand in one yard or another, chatting. In the winter, though, we hardly saw our neighbors. We did what most Wisconsinites do in the winter. We hunkered down in our houses and waited for the cold to pass so we could catch up and maybe even gossip a little come springtime.

After receiving a cancer diagnosis in October, I underwent surgery in November and received treatment throughout the winter. So, I was surprised when one of my neighbors, Janean, approached me in March.

"Some neighbors have been talking and we would like to do something to help you, but we need ideas of things you need done. We can come clean for you or do yard work or whatever else will help you and the kids."

I was at a loss for words. "Wow. Thanks."

"I don't want to put you on the spot but think about what would be helpful for you and I'll reconnect with you next week."

For my entire life, I had insisted on taking care of everything myself. I didn't want to be a burden, and I didn't want others to think I was lazy or incompetent. I valued independence, hard work, and strength. I had spent my whole life taking care of myself and others and it would be fair to say that I derived my self-worth from that ability. Having taken care of everything for so long, I didn't even know what to ask my neighbors to do. I was sure I didn't want my entire neighborhood in my house to see what a mess it was, but that meant I needed to figure out what else they could do to help us. In the end, I told Janean I didn't know what to ask for, but if they wanted to do outside work, that would be awesome. She said, "Great! Got it!"

On a sunny day in April, I looked outside, and my yard was full of people. They did all the things that need to be done every spring in Wisconsin when the world begins to turn green. They power washed my house and cleaned all of my windows. They did yard work and took care of my flowerbeds. They even did some work in my garage. Some of the people in my yard I knew well and some I hardly knew at all, but they all wanted to help us and I was in awe of their generosity. My eyes welled up with tears as I watched out the window.

That day, as I watched my neighbors, I realized people love helping those who have hit a tough patch. Those neighbors were not judging me; they were just helping me to get through a challenging time. They were lifting me up until I could do the same for someone else.

I learned that when people offer to help, they aren't doing it because they think you can't take care of yourself; they are doing it because they care about you. I am so grateful for all the people who reached out to me and my family. I find it impossible to imagine my cancer journey without every single person who signed up and brought a meal for me and my kids. It took us months to eat all of them, but I didn't have to feel guilty because I didn't have the energy to make a meal for my children. Every one of those women in recovery who helped me by making sure I got a meeting, sitting by my side at the hospital, or just being there for me when I needed a friend, is also an important part of my story. And I am still grateful to the neighbors who gave of their most valuable resource, time, to make my life a bit brighter. I will probably always struggle with asking for help. I think that's in my DNA. Cancer taught me, though, that strength sometimes looks like admitting you can't do everything alone, and there is no shame in that.

# Chapter 22

# I Am More Than My Body Parts

"Body love is more than acceptance of self or the acceptance of the body. Body love is about self-worth in general. It's more than our physical appearance.
Mary Lambert

In kindergarten, I could not sit "like a pretzel" on the floor. I was tall and awkward. My classmates made fun of me all the way through elementary school because I was so skinny, and I had knobby knees. Like the average overweight American, what I wouldn't give to be that thin today.

In fifth grade, there was a shift. I wish I could say that was when I began to feel like I fit in, when my classmates stopped making fun of me because of my appearance. Nope. It was the year I got boobs. I was one of the first in my class to develop, and this was not a welcome evolution. With it, I stopped being the skinny girl and became the girl with boobs. All the unwanted attention on my body that began in fifth grade might be where my own difficulty with body image and self-worth really took root.

By seventh grade, I had reached my full adult height of five foot eight, and I tipped the scales at 130 pounds. I was still skinny, but the only thing the boys noticed now was my boobs. In junior high, I was the only girl wearing a C-cup bra. It is safe to say "the girls" were my most prominent feature. No matter how many times I read the young adult novel, *Are You There God? It's Me Margaret,* I never once did exercises to increase the size of my breasts. That was the last thing I wanted.

In seventh grade, I joined the basketball team. Every time I ran down the court, I was reminded of these two giant blobs on my chest. If you weren't "gifted" with large breasts, you may not realize what an issue this is. To put it simply, running was painful. When I purchased sports bras for my daughters in the early 2000s, these amazing, beautiful pieces of craftsmanship amazed me. They had vertical, horizontal, and diagonal support. This was not a thing in the late seventies and early eighties. No matter what sports bra I tried, the result was the same. My large breasts ached with every step and every bounce. I longed to be more like my teammates. I'm pretty sure that regardless of what else they felt when they ran, they did not feel like their boobs were being torn from their bodies.

Our school colors were purple and white. For away games we wore the purple uniforms and for home games we wore white. I had a teammate who would arrive in the locker room to get dressed for home games only to exclaim, "I need to call my mom. I forgot my bra again!" Seriously?! There was not a moment in my life post-fifth grade where I could forget my bra. It was as essential as my shoes and contact lenses. Of course, we all laughed every time; it was funny. But I was also jealous. Basketball would be so much easier if I could just get rid of these hindrances on my chest. It would be decades before I would remember the statement "Be careful what you wish for."

The teasing was constant through most of junior high and high school. Teenage boys are merciless and sometimes cruel, and they are unapologetic in their quest to objectify women. All they care about, it seems, is that their friends think they are funny.

They threw things down the front of my shirt, and they unhooked my bra as they sat behind me in English class. I suppose they called it "practice." And that was only the beginning. In the seventies and early eighties, tube tops and halter tops were popular, and there were no school rules against wearing them. Once when I wore one, I was the victim of a boy who thought he was hilarious. He untied my halter top and as it fell, I grabbed it around my chest and raced into the girl's bathroom. I was mortified. I thought I might never come out of that stall, but of course, that wasn't an option. I tied the halter top in a double knot and when I came out, all I heard was laughter. I can tell you now, as someone who taught high school for twenty-eight years, a lot of the kids laughing didn't think it was funny. They just didn't want to be the target, so they laughed. At the time, I was humiliated. This was complicated by the fact that I was an introvert. I talked endlessly, hoping to bury my vulnerability, but inside, I was just a sensitive teen girl. Their teasing jabs stung, leaving me with a desire to disappear. This happened almost daily because, unfortunately, my boobs were a constant source of amusement to my peers.

It wasn't until twenty-six years later, when one of those boys called to make amends to me for how he treated me in high school, that anyone divulged the disgusting fact that those boys had created a "Best Boobs" list for our graduating class. Yup! Me, my best friend, and one other girl topped the list. My former classmate still somehow thought that I should see that as a compliment. I didn't. It was offensive in 1983, and it was still offensive in 2009. By the age of forty-five, though, I had become accustomed to having large breasts and so it was no longer a source of humiliation. In case you haven't caught up yet, though, objectifying women (or anyone for that matter) is a shitty thing to do. If it had only been immature high school boy stuff, it would have passed, but a lot of men are just teenage boys in the bodies of grown men.

I was in my late twenties and had a part-time job at JCPenney. I worked in the men's department right next to the shoe department. Often, I had to transfer merchandise from my department to their desk. That is where Robert enters the story. He was a young twenty-something who worked in the shoe department. Every time I went over to the desk, we would have a brief cordial conversation and every time, without fail, the entire conversation took place with him staring straight at my chest. Every time, until the day that I had finally had enough. I had withstood years of comments, catcalls walking down the street, and men's eyes on my boobs. Without thinking, I reached out, placed my index finger under his chin, and as I lifted his chin, I said, "My eyes are up here." I will give Robert this: It was the last time I ever caught him talking to my boobs.

During my life, I got used to this, but I never liked it. I learned to laugh along, though, and sometimes I even liked the attention my boobs garnered. Still, I never felt comfortable with it, and there were still times I thought life would have been so much simpler without those orbs on my chest.

Fast forward to just months before my diagnosis. Cade and I were discussing breast reduction surgery. My best friend from high school—yes, one of the "Best Boobs" vote getters—had this surgery, so I knew a little something about it. As I mentioned earlier, Cade was scandalized that women do that. I explained how difficult it can be to carry them around and how some women have horrible back problems from carrying the weight. This is when he said, "I'll help you carry them." Yes, it was a joke. But was it? I have often questioned whether any guy I dated loved me or just had an infatuation with my boobs, as my boobs seemed to occupy more of my boyfriends' attention than anything else about me.

People often tell me, "If I were diagnosed with breast cancer, I would just tell them to cut them off. I've hated them my whole life." To this day, it bothers me when people are so dismissive of the topic, but I understand that it isn't real until it becomes our own personal experience. If I had ever considered the possibility of being diagnosed with breast cancer, I might have said the same thing. When it's your reality and not a hypothetical scenario, however, it is different. I did not feel like telling them to "just cut them off" when I received the news that I had cancer, and it was still not where I was emotionally the day I decided that the best choice for me was to have a bilateral mastectomy.

I was distraught. I believed no one would ever find me attractive again. I was certain Cade would leave me and no one else would want me either. Why would anyone want someone so ugly? I have thought about this often since having cancer. I hide behind the perception of being strong and independent, but the truth is, vulnerability terrifies me. My whole life I've been afraid that if I let someone in, they will not like the real me and eventually they will leave. How could I possibly withstand that kind of pain? My self-esteem has been tenuous since I was a child. Looking back, I think this is why the teasing when I was a teenager was so difficult, but it still doesn't fully explain why losing my boobs was so traumatic or why I thought not having boobs meant I was ugly. For that, I had to dig a little deeper.

As I have reflected since my cancer diagnosis, what I realized is that I have let others determine my identity and worth my whole life rather than feeling an innate sense of self-worth. It started as a little girl, and those things I experienced during puberty and adolescence just magnified it. All those boys and men during my lifetime who focused their attention on my boobs reinforced my opinion that I was not enough. I was nothing more than what I could offer someone else and all I could offer was this: a pair of nice boobs. Looking back, it makes me sad to see how little I thought of myself.

I am smart and while I'm not what I would call beautiful, I am not unattractive. I am conscientious, honest, and compassionate. I care about and take care of people; I love kids and animals; and I will fight injustice wherever I see it. There is so much more to me than my body parts. For so many years, I let other people define who I was, and I didn't even see it happening. As a result, when facing breast cancer, I felt like I was losing who I was as a woman. Society's expectations and the relentless messages from advertisers and social media only further convinced me that happiness was impossible without breasts.

Despite everything, I understand that no one else gave me low self-esteem. That came from me. My perception and the facts are not the same thing. Years ago, I was talking to a male friend from high school. I told him I always felt bullied and ostracized in school because I was smart and because of my body. He said, "No. Everybody liked you. They made fun of me because I wasn't smart." He had an amazing personality, and all the girls thought he was attractive. Because he didn't do well in school, his perception was that he didn't fit in. Interesting, isn't it? We are all fighting our own battles, but we don't need to let them define us.

Today I know I am more than the sum of my parts. I am married to a wonderful man who sees so many positive qualities in me and not even one of them has to do with any of my body parts or lack thereof. And, ultimately, this is not important. It's nice, but what is nicer is that *I* don't define myself by my body parts. I'm still a work in progress. I still spend too much time in front of the mirror trying to hide my wrinkles and other minor imperfections, but I spend more time working on being a good person, on keeping "my side of the street clean," being kind to others, apologizing when I'm wrong, and living my life so that I don't have to apologize as often.

My experience with cancer has contributed to this personal growth. Sure, I have implants, and I have numbness across my breasts, but it is not a factor in my life today. I don't think about my boobs one way or the other, and I doubt I would even notice if someone were staring at them. I am content with who I am today, and I don't have to look in a mirror or have someone comment on my appearance to feel good about myself. I am more than my body parts.

# Chapter 23

# Love Is Being There for Each Other

"Perhaps the greatest test of love is the way we act in times of need."
Suleika Jaouad, *Between Two Kingdoms*

I couldn't come up with another way to say it, except to look directly at him, take a deep breath and blurt out, "I have breast cancer." Cade looked at me briefly before looking down at his hands and then back at me. He took a deep breath and with a nervous half-hearted laugh said, "I wasn't expecting that."

I watched him expectantly. For what, I'm not sure. Tears clouded my vision as he wrapped his arms around me and said, "You will beat this, hon. There is no other option."

Two days went by before Cade spoke again about my cancer, and even then, it wasn't the response I had anticipated. We were sitting at my kitchen table when he told me he had been contemplating ending our relationship. It was not his first time admitting that to me.

What the hell? I thought. I just told you I have cancer and you are going to walk out on me?

Before I could say anything, he continued, "I think this is my Higher Power telling me this is where I'm supposed to be and that we are supposed to fight this together."

That day in my kitchen, I heard him saying God was telling him we were meant to be together. It would be a long time before I heard his words for what they really were.

During my first marriage and prior to my sobriety, I built walls so high and so strong that when I got sober, I knew it would take time and work to tear them down. Cade was a big part of that process of letting someone in. I met him in recovery and foolishly started dating him before I had time to do any real work on myself. We attended meetings together, we enjoyed motorcycle rides on sunny days, we shared a unique sense of humor, and his friends, all in recovery, became our friends.

From Cade, I learned about recovery from alcoholism and more about how to be in a healthy relationship. Our relationship was far from perfect, but compared to my marriage, which I left three months before I quit drinking, it seemed blissful to me. Or maybe I was seeing what I wanted to see.

About a year into the relationship, when he told me he thought we should go our separate ways. I was blindsided, and I couldn't imagine my life without him in it. Sitting on his couch as the tears fell, I begged him to give us a chance. Today, I would call my behavior that night and in the days that followed emotional manipulation; at the time, I did not have any other tools at my disposal, other than the unfair fighting I had resorted to in previous relationships. After a few days, Cade agreed to give our relationship a chance.

After that, I suspected he was "exploring his options." Every time those thoughts popped into my head, though, I pushed them down, convincing myself it was me overthinking things again. Some low-level gaslighting on his part played a part in this as well. One time, as I was asking repeated questions about a female friend, he snapped, "You need to stop blaming me for your ex-husband's behavior. I am not him!" That was a red flag, but I was blind to it. This wasn't the first time a guy tried to make me feel like I was imagining things, like I was the one who was crazy. I guess it's a great cover if you know you aren't doing the right thing. Today, I understand it for what it is. A form of abuse.

Things didn't change; they just got worse. There were more and more clues that he was not being faithful to our relationship. I learned in recovery to focus on myself and make sure I was doing "the next right thing," but I started to engage in unhealthy patterns again. I knew Cade's passwords, and I checked his Facebook messenger and his text messages daily. Somewhere in my mind, I believed that understanding the situation would give me power over the result. This became an obsession.

When I told him about the cancer, part of me thought this would be a good excuse for him to bail, and, at the same time, I hoped maybe he would realize how much he loved me and stay. I know this sounds like the thoughts of an immature teenager or someone who has read far too many romance novels. I didn't say it made sense. It's amazing how our brains can do cartwheels to convince us we are meant to be in a relationship that isn't meant to be. When Cade told me he believed his Higher Power was calling on him to be here for me, I believed we would work all of this out together. That, more than anything, was what I wanted to be true at that moment.

There were additional red flags, though. The day of my surgery when he didn't say we had our whole lives ahead of us and instead said I needed to get through this "for my kids," I knew he was trying not to give me false hope, but like all the other clues, I just dismissed it because it didn't fit with the narrative I was creating in my head.

This was no longer a healthy relationship, if it had ever been; in fact, for me it was toxic. Throughout my entire cancer journey, Cade chatted with other women. His behavior was becoming less acceptable, and so was mine. I monitored his phone and even deleted questionable text messages from women. My thoughts became erratic. I convinced myself that with everything we had been through together, I needed to make this work. That sounds crazy even as I type it. One person cannot make a relationship work. I was not in my right mind.

I was not a victim; not really. In recovery, we talk about the -ism. This is what you are left with when you take the alcohol out of the alcoholic. What remains is the -ism portion of alcoholism. These are all of the character defects that we used to manage with drinking. I had many -isms and most of them were based on fear and my belief that if I could just control the people and events around me, I would be safe and happy. I played a part in this toxic relationship. Neither one of us were doing "the next right thing."

Cade was not always a good boyfriend, but he was a good person. He was there for every step of my cancer journey. It was Cade who sat in the hospital during my six-hour mastectomy, and when they had to admit me to the hospital that night, he slept on a couch in the room with me. He was there, cracking jokes for the benefit of my kids, who must have been terrified to see their mom so weak; he supported me as I struggled to walk to the end of the hall so I could go home; and he helped me up the stairs and organized my pain pills next to my chair, complete with a log sheet so I wouldn't take too many. Cade even made sure Abbey knew how to help me with my drain tubes before he left to work his overnight shift.

Every night for the first couple weeks, Cade came home from work, kneeled by my chair, and stroked my hair. He looked into my eyes, asked how I was feeling, and told me he loved me. I was in incredible pain and for several days he slept on the loveseat in my living room until moving to the bedroom so he could finally get some quality sleep.

One morning, he came home and admitted to me that he had passed out at work and had to be checked out at the hospital. Being the caretaker of someone with cancer is hard work. It is scary and stressful and often thankless. Cade and Abbey shared this role. They helped me shower and dress for the first several weeks, emptied my drain tubes, and made sure I ate. He needed to take care of himself too, and I encouraged him to do so. Once I recuperated from the surgery, Cade was able to resume some aspects of his own life, such as spending time at his own house. However, I found it challenging to cope with the emotional effects of my surgery and the additional insecurity that arose because I was dating a man whose commitment was uncertain, which at times caused me to feel incapacitated. Still, Cade was there for me as much as he could be.

The things Cade did that weren't related to my cancer were perhaps even more significant, at least for me. My son Hunter had a girlfriend; he found places to escape to because that's what he needed to do. Abbey, though, took on responsibility for my caretaking, and Cade tried to relieve her of that stress in a million different ways. He distracted her with humor, he took her on short motorcycle rides, and he taught her important life skills, like how to pick a lock. That statement probably requires a little explanation. Abbey wanted to go with Cade to help build a shed at his mom's house. He needed a tool he didn't bring with, but his mom wasn't home, so he tried to pick the lock to get into her house. Of course, the first thing she said when she came home was, "Cade taught me how to pick a lock today." To this day, Abbey remembers with fondness her relationship with Cade. She even invited him to her high school graduation. I will always be grateful that he was there to give her a little time to be a kid.

As I approached the end of my cancer treatment, things grew increasingly strained in my relationship with Cade. I was pretty sure the end was near. Suddenly, though, he decided we should look at houses. He lived thirty-two miles away—from my house, from his job, and from most of his recovery meetings. He wanted to look at houses closer to all of those things. We looked at a couple and I gained optimism for the future as he asked me hypothetical questions about my drive from the property we were viewing to my job and the kids' activities.

It was a surprise, then, when I checked his email a couple of days later. Yes, I was still doing that; it had become my newest addiction. He had emailed a woman from a dating site, asking the general "get to know you" kinds of questions. I was pissed, and I was hurt. Then why the hell was I wasting my time looking at houses with him? Instead of dealing with this as a reasonable adult might, I emailed her from his account, telling her we had been in a relationship for over two years and were, in fact, looking at houses. I thought that was the end of it until she sent him a scathing email back. Of course, I had to delete the email so he would not discover I had been breaking into his email. Real mature! I know.Unfortunately, that was not the only woman he was talking to. Just a couple weeks later, Cade took a phone call while I was with him. He walked away from me to have the conversation. After he hung up, I asked, "Who was that?"

"Kyle," he said.

"Who's Kyle?"

"Just a guy from work."

It just didn't feel right, so the next day after he went to work, I logged into our cell phone account, and there was a phone number that kept showing up. I called it and when the woman on the other end of the line answered, I asked, "Who is this?"

She said, "Lisa. Who are you?"

"My name is Angela and I'm pretty sure you have been chatting with Cade Johnson. I wanted you to know that he's in a relationship and when you called yesterday, he told me you were Kyle, so apparently you are a secret."

With that, I heard a click on the other end of the line. I knew I was in trouble. I had never actually called any of the women I thought he was talking to, and I didn't doubt for a second that she would tell him I called.

Later that night I tried to log into the cell phone account again, but I got an "invalid password" error message. It was obvious that he had locked me out. I spent the rest of the night trying to figure out how I could explain myself to salvage what little was left of our relationship.

I didn't have to worry about what I was going to say because when he came back to my house after his work shift, he looked at me calmly and said, "I'm done. This is over." With that, he turned around and walked out of my house. I didn't even attempt to respond. There was no point. He was justifiably angry with me and I'm sure he believed I had gone off the deep end. From my side of things, I thought he should take responsibility for his behavior. While he did have a lot to take responsibility for, so did I, and I wasn't ready to take responsibility for my actions either.

The onslaught of thoughts and emotions this breakup triggered caught me off guard. My friends were "our friends" and many were initially his friends. Our social life revolved around recovery and now we needed to navigate that separately. It appeared to come more easily to him than it did to me. My vindictive side surfaced as he attended events with the woman he was pursuing when he broke up with me. I was angry, and I sent her a letter detailing what I viewed as his history of cheating. My sponsor insisted I make amends to him. I found this to be infuriating since I was busy acting my part as the victim. She also recommended that it might not be productive for me to make these amends in person, so my instructions were to write him a letter apologizing for my part without mentioning what I perceived as his part. It sucked, but I did it because I wanted to stay sober.

Dr. Adebayo declared me cancer-free, but I was struggling. My anger was bubbling just below the surface, and I was on the edge of tears most days. That day in Dr. Adebayo's office I slipped right over the edge and found myself sobbing. I was a mess, but I had not taken a drink. I was determined that if I could survive a battle with cancer without drinking, I was not going to screw that up now. I no longer had cancer, but I was far from healed. Chemotherapy was over, but this was the beginning of my healing process, from both the trauma of cancer and from relying too much on others for my sense of self-worth.

Later, after some time spent in therapy grieving the loss of what I envisioned might be and learning how to love myself instead of relying on men for my value, I started to gain some perspective. I had accumulated a wealth of experience with infidelity. My first husband was unfaithful during most of our twenty-plus years together, so when Cade exhibited similar behaviors, I was easily triggered. As part of that entire journey, there were instances when both of them manipulated me, causing me to question my own perception. I also took time to confront my own problematic behaviors in relationships. Like I said, I started dating Cade before I should have. There is a reason they caution you in recovery against dating anyone for at least a year. It is important to work on yourself first. I was finally doing that work three years into recovery.

I realized that I would never tolerate cheating or gaslighting again. When I met the man that I am now married to just months after the breakup, it didn't take long to figure out things were going to need to be different. Glenn told me, early in our relationship, that I was going to have to trust him if this relationship was going anywhere. That was it. I decided to do things differently, and a year later, he proposed.

I had taken a new job and moved, and two years after finishing my cancer treatment, I returned to my old stomping grounds and attended a meeting. It was my intent to pick up my five-year sobriety chip where I first got sober. I shared a little about my journey at that meeting, as well as the fact that I was now engaged and the happiest I had ever been.

Cade was at that meeting and following the meeting he asked if he could talk to me. He apologized to me for what he now referred to as his "cheating behavior." It was nice that he made those amends, but it changed nothing for me. I have learned over the years I have been sober that amends are for the person making them, not the one receiving them. I had spent the past couple of years working on myself and I no longer needed him to admit to those behaviors in order to believe I deserved to be treated well. The truth is that neither one of us treated the other as we should have.

This seemed like the official conclusion of a chapter in my life, but in truth, I had already closed that book a long time ago. I was in an amazing relationship with a man I trusted implicitly, and I had way too much self-respect now to allow myself to be treated like someone's second choice ever again.

When I arrived back home and looked at my phone, I had a text from Cade. It said, "Congratulations on both your five years of sobriety and your engagement. Love always, Cade." At the time, the message felt inappropriate to me, but today I understand it. "I love you" doesn't always mean what you think it means or what you'd like it to mean. It has been over a decade now since this relationship ended and I have had time and distance to process everything that took place. As I was preparing to write this chapter, I considered that relationship and it looks a lot different to me now than it did then.

Cade and I have not seen or talked to each other in many years, but I do believe that in that season of life we loved each other. That does not mean we were meant to be in a long-lasting, committed relationship. If that was our destiny, we would have made it happen; we would have fought for it. As much as I thought I was fighting for "us," that is not what I was doing. Our relationship was healthier than previous relationships I had been in, but in the end, it was still unhealthy.

Despite all of that, the relationship had its foundation in love. No one gives up six months of their life to act as caretaker for a cancer patient on a whim. I know Cade loved me. He loved me enough to want to see me through the scariest time of my life; he cared about me enough to make it a little easier for me to make that journey sober. Perhaps most importantly to me, he cared enough about my kids to want to be there for them.

When our relationship ended, I convinced myself he was leaving because of my cancer. The truth is exactly what he told me when I told him I had been diagnosed with cancer: "I think this is my Higher Power telling me this is where I'm supposed to be and that we are supposed to fight this together." He didn't leave because of my cancer; he stayed because of my cancer. He never told me he would stay forever. That is what I heard because I wanted it to be true, not because it was true.

Cade and I will always have a connection that I will never have with another living soul outside of my family. He was my rock during my cancer battle. I leaned on him. He held me up when I couldn't stand on my own physically, and he was there to hold me when I needed to cry because there was nothing else I could do. I am sure I could have made it through cancer without him, but I don't know what that would have looked like. I will always be thankful he stayed and acted as my caretaker. And yes, I will always love him for that. It is this I remember today, not the poor decisions he made or the equally terrible decisions I made.

People come into our lives for a reason. And sometimes they leave, but it is okay because the lessons stay. I learned so much from this relationship. I learned I can't make the behaviors of another human being go away by making worse decisions myself; I learned I'm not in control of the outcome of any situation; and I learned some people are in our lives for a season, and they were never meant to stay forever. Mostly, I learned love takes many forms and sometimes it was never what we thought it was, but that doesn't mean it wasn't love.

# Chapter 24

---

# I Am a Work in Progress

"The greatest glory in living lies not in never falling, but in rising every time we fall."
Nelson Mandela

After my breakup with Cade and my last appointment with Dr. Adebayo, I started taking depression meds in conjunction with attending more recovery meetings. Within a couple of weeks, I was feeling a little better; at least I wasn't crying all the time. I don't know how much of that to attribute to the meds, but I hated the idea that I needed medication to function like a reasonable adult. I couldn't escape that little voice in the back of my head telling me I was weak; I should be able to do this on my own.

On the plus side (or so I thought at the time), one of the side effects of these meds was potential weight loss. When I sat down to eat, after a few bites, I was done. Eating more than that made me nauseous. The weight melted off my body. I lost 45 pounds in four weeks, and I sure wasn't going to complain about that! I know. That kind of thinking is not good. It was obsessive and unhealthy. I had been overweight for decades, though, and feeling unattractive following the cancer and the break-up with Cade, my broken brain told me that if I lost weight, I might be attractive and desirable again. This disordered eating was a result of my disordered thinking.

I had scheduled an appointment with the therapist as Dr. Adebayo recommended, and as it neared, I couldn't help thinking, I'm feeling better. Maybe I don't really need therapy. These are the lies my broken brain tells me. Fortunately, I have friends who have been in therapy for decades. They assured me I did indeed need therapy, so I went to the appointment, certain that it would be one appointment, and the therapist would tell me I didn't need to come back. Have I mentioned my brain is broken at times?

I had been to therapy in the past, but that was right after I quit drinking and that time we focused on my alcoholism. This time would turn out to be different. As we started the session, the therapist asked me what brought me to therapy.

"Well, when you cry in the oncologist's office after he tells you that you are cancer-free and they aren't tears of joy, he gifts you with antidepressants and a referral to therapy."

Shawna, the therapist, expressed concern about my depression. She asked if I remembered ever feeling like this in the past; I did not. Then she asked questions more related to anxiety. The things she asked about on the anxiety screening pretty much summed up how I had felt ever since I was a child. Trouble falling or staying asleep, tension headaches, fatigue, trouble focusing, trouble making decisions, unable to relax. It was almost like she already knew me.

She asked me if I was familiar with PTSD (post-traumatic stress disorder). I had heard of it. She continued, "Most people associate PTSD with soldiers in the military, typically those who are deployed, but it can occur after any traumatic event."

"Okay?"

"We have seen it following things like 9/11 and the Oklahoma City Bombing, but also after things like witnessing a murder or surviving a sexual assault. It can also happen after things like a battle with cancer."

"So you think I have PTSD?"

"I think it's too early to make that diagnosis, but I think it makes sense that you have been experiencing anxiety and depression following your cancer. It is your body's trauma response."

I wanted her to just tell me what was wrong with me and fix it so I could move on. "So what is wrong with me, and how do we fix it?"

"For now, I am comfortable with a diagnosis of generalized anxiety. I would like you to stay on the medication and we will get you scheduled for another appointment next week." I guess my friends were right. This would not be a one and done therapy visit.

At my next visit, we talked about the anxiety that had been present in my life for as long as I could remember. I had always struggled with fear and uneasiness. I had dedicated a significant portion of my life to coping with my insecurity and experiencing a sense of not fitting in anywhere. I was a textbook example of an overthinker. I worried about things far beyond my control and attempted to manipulate those situations, which, naturally, proved impossible and intensified my preoccupation with them. I had always operated with low-grade anxiety and I just managed it. None of this had ever appeared troublesome to me. I was sure everyone had these thoughts and feelings, so I did my best to handle it myself.

According to Shawna, "It sounds like operating in survival mode has been a major part of your life." She looked at me, gauging my reaction. "It doesn't have to be this difficult, Angela."

Thus began the journey of determining where my anxiety came from and what made it worse, how I had been managing it, and how I could better manage it. I liked this therapist; she was easy to talk to, and I didn't feel like she was trying to put me on meds and leave me there. Shawna asked questions about my childhood, my alcoholism, and my cancer. Gradually, we began to see a link between grief and an increase in the level of my anxiety. Shawna cited my alcoholism as an example. I struggled at the beginning of my recovery, and I had sought therapy.

Shawna said, "There is a grieving process involved in recovering from addiction. You know that the substance is harmful to you. You understand it is ruining your life, but you feel its absence; you mourn the loss."

I am certain that is true. To this day, I sometimes reminisce about the feeling of enjoying a cold beer on a scorching summer day or how much more effortless it became to mingle with unfamiliar individuals after consuming a few drinks or how easy it was to dull my emotions with alcohol. Of course, these things came at a cost to me, but that didn't mean I didn't grieve the loss of alcohol. It had been my best friend. It had been my solution until it became my problem.

That revelation prompted me to question what I was grieving now that I had reached the end of my cancer treatment. We spent some time on this question. I felt like this was the key to unlocking my anxiety and depression.

Did I mourn the loss of my breasts? The very breasts I once wished I didn't have? The breasts that served as a source of humiliation in high school? The answer was yes. Somehow, the transformation of losing my breasts led me to believe that I was less of a woman. Did I feel sadness because of the loss of a relationship? That was also true. I had been aware for a long time that this relationship might not survive, but I had still convinced myself that Cade was my lifelong partner. I had perceived my cancer as the element that would grant us such resilience as a couple that no obstacle could overcome us, an idea that was never within the realm of possibility.

In the end, this grief was complex, as most grief is. Grieving conventional losses such as death is commonplace, but how was I supposed to grieve the loss of a body part, much less nonessential ones such as my boobs? There was no funeral service, no closure at all. I went to sleep in the hospital with two breasts and I woke up with none. I did not want the scars and the implants, but mostly I just didn't want to be different. I didn't feel whole.

My breasts had been a source of unwanted attention, but in the end, that had somehow made them a part of my identity. My identity as a woman was wrapped up in those two globes of fat. It makes sense. This patriarchal society of ours places an absurd value on them. Men stare at them, they make lewd comments about them, and they tell jokes about them. On a more serious note, though, these two boobs fed all my babies, and all of my children snuggled into them to seek comfort, so in that way my womanhood was tied to them.

Like a lot of survivors, I vacillated between gratitude that my cancer was gone and grief for what else I had lost with it. In therapy, I learned I needed to allow myself to grieve. It was okay to be angry, and it was okay to be sad. Eventually, I would accept the loss of my breasts, along with all the other changes in my life because of long-term side effects from the chemotherapy. I would even be able to share my experience with others openly and honestly to make their journey a little less difficult. This came after a lot of therapy, though, and the passage of time.

I also was grieving the loss of a relationship that had been important to me. The fact that Cade broke up with me at the end of this cancer battle left me with an impression that it was all about how cancer altered my appearance, making me feel unwanted and undesirable. My overthinking brain translated that into "if this person I had history with doesn't find me desirable, then no one will." My life experience, along with cancer and mastectomy, left me feeling like I had nothing else to offer. I now realize how horribly sad and misguided that is, but it took a lot of therapy and a solid relationship with someone who did not know me before cancer to get me there.

Losing this relationship for me symbolized a loss of my self-worth. The bigger issue was that my self-worth never should have been wrapped up in another person in the first place. That was old thinking. When I was a child, if someone was mad at me, I thought that meant I was unlovable; as a teen and young adult, I thought everything the people around me did or said somehow reflected on me, and my self-esteem was wrapped up in what I believed they thought about me. I was insecure, but what a big ego I had. Recovery and therapy have taught me that the entire world does not, in fact, revolve around me. This doesn't mean that I don't still struggle with these thoughts today, but I now have tools to help me navigate them. I can pause. I can ask, What are you telling yourself? I can slow down and breathe because "this too shall pass."

I continued therapy for several months and I stayed on the meds for some time beyond that. Since then, I have gained confidence in my ability to handle difficult situations. Once I get through a crisis, though, I may relapse a bit. This happened during the pandemic in 2020. I dealt with the actual pandemic and the lockdown pretty well. When we all returned to school for the 2020–2021 school year, that was another story. My anxiety flared like a fire in a windstorm. This time I didn't wait, though. One of the lessons I learned from the depression following my cancer journey was that therapy would help me—but I had to reach out. This time I wasn't starting from the beginning, but there was still work to do.

I wish I could say all of this inner work has fixed everything in my life, but it hasn't. I worked through the grief and developed a deeper understanding of my brain and how anxiety and fear affected my thought patterns, but I still get upset, frustrated, and anxious sometimes. I still have that same broken brain and I haven't quite figured out that I don't have to do everything myself, that I don't always have to be strong for everyone around me, and that instead of putting up my wall during traumatic seasons in my life, maybe I need to lower the wall. Maybe I need to let people in and maybe I need to seek therapy *during* the battle instead of waiting to fall apart at the end. At the end of the day, though, I keep traveling this world called life "one day at a time."

# Chapter 25

# Do Not Regret the Past

"To regret one's own experiences is to arrest one's own development. To deny one's own experiences is to put a lie into the lips of one's own life. It is no less than a denial of the soul."
Oscar Wilde

"What if?" Two of the most anxiety-provoking words in the English language. I dedicated a significant amount of time pondering my battle with cancer, fixated on the idea that the past could have taken a different course if I had made different choices. Let me explain. I am not delusional. There was no other course of action I could have taken to prevent a cancer diagnosis or needing surgery. I wish I had done more to make this easier on my kids, though.

It started right at the beginning. My eldest daughter suspected that something was off when she kept asking for the results, and I kept telling her I had not yet been notified. It was my belief that Hunter should finish the run of his school play without the stress of my diagnosis affecting him, and I reasoned that minimizing the kids' concerns would benefit everyone.

I spent a lot of time later wondering if I had been protecting them or if my fear caused the delay. Was it self-serving? Or was I acting in the best interest of my kids? I looked back and saw the stress that I put Rae under. For a while, I justified the decision. She would not have been able to process without talking to her siblings, but maybe I owed her the chance. In the end, it doesn't matter. I made the decision I made. It is our reality. There is nothing I can do to change it now, and I wasn't in a good enough head space to ask these questions at the time.

One of my biggest regrets was the result of my chemotherapy and its effect on my body: In the middle of treatment, at the height of my fatigue and brain fog, I arrived at the clinic on Friday for my regularly scheduled chemotherapy. The nurse hooked up my port to run the pretreatment blood work, and I waited. Soon, she came out to the waiting room.

"How has your fatigue been?" she asked.

"Well, it's there."

"Are you weak? More tired than usual?"

"I'm okay. Why?"

"Your red blood cell counts are low. We can do a blood transfusion today and then resume treatment in a week. That would give the cells a chance to regenerate. What are your thoughts?"

I did *not* want to delay the end of chemo. I had an end date in my head and the thought of extending that made me want to cry.

"I'm fine. Let's just do the treatment and see what next week brings."

Flash forward four days to my return to work. I stepped out of my car, and a wave of fatigue met me. I reached out, putting my hand on my car to steady myself. It will be fine, I thought as I walked to the door. I can do this. When I reached my classroom, I dropped into my chair and turned on my computer.

As I clicked through four days' worth of emails, Beth walked in the door with an animated, "Good morning. I have your tea."

This sophomore angel stopped at the coffee shop every other Wednesday and bought a chamomile tea for me. The first time she did it, she said, "I heard chamomile tea is supposed to help settle your stomach; I hope it works."

Beth did not always receive acceptance from her peers, but her kind heart and the tea she brought me filled me with appreciation.

I taught mostly from my chair these days, but today still seemed worse than normal. My head was pulsing, and I closed my eyes to shut out the noisy world. I rested my elbow on the desk, holding my head up, more than usual, and the ache in my neck made me wish I could just put my head down on my desk and take a nap. It was only nine thirty in the morning, and sleeping was not an option with a room full of sixteen-year-olds. I struggled to keep my eyes open, waiting for the end of the class period and my prep.

Once the halls emptied and period two started, I made the long trek to the teacher's work room to get my mail. It had been a long walk for me for weeks now, but today was something else. I could take only six or seven steps at a time before needing to lean against the lockers. I didn't know how I was going to get through this day without someone to push me around in a wheelchair. It had to be ten minutes later when I finally arrived in the work room and collapsed onto one of the couches around the perimeter of the room. If I could just lie down for a few minutes, maybe this would pass.

I had just closed my eyes when I felt something touch me. I jumped, looking around the room as I tried to regain my bearings. Karen, an administrative assistant from the front office, had seen me on the couch and she had grown concerned. If anyone ever tells you the administrative assistants at schools are there to answer phones and deliver messages, they don't know what they are talking about. These women are the heartbeat of the school. They take care of all of us, students and staff, every single day. The place could not function without them and they deserve a significant increase in pay.

"Angela ... Angela. Are you okay?"

"Oh." I pushed myself to a sitting position. "I am just so tired." I looked at the clock to see that twenty minutes had passed. "I better call the clinic."

The nurse I spoke to on the phone didn't hesitate to tell me I should come in as soon as possible for a blood transfusion. I stopped in the office and told them I needed to go to the clinic. Those amazing ladies, of course, would find someone to cover my classes for the rest of the day. So, I trudged back down the long hallway, grabbed my bag and my keys, and drove myself to the hospital. I'm sure you see the issue here, but it never occurred to me until they asked me at the end of the transfusion if I had someone there with me. Nope, it was not a good idea for me to drive in the condition I was in. Fortunately, I made it to the hospital without hurting myself or anyone else, and soon they had me hooked up to an IV and I awaited the infusion of someone else's blood.

I learned a couple of things about blood transfusions that day. It turns out you can be allergic to someone else's blood. Before starting the infusion, the nurse said, "In very rare instances, you can have a reaction to the blood, so if you feel any itching or are having difficulty breathing, let us know right away." No problem. Yes, problem. Midway through the first bag of blood, my arm started to itch a little. I turned my arm over and there it was, one single hive.

"How are you doing so far?"

"I think I might have the beginnings of some hives." I showed her.

She grabbed the phone and the next thing I heard was, "Dr. Adebayo. Call 2201. Possible anaphylaxis."

What? It's one little hive, I thought as I heard her repeat the call. I felt like I had teleported into an episode of *Grey's Anatomy*. My curiosity sparked, and I awaited what would unfold next. In came the nurse with a syringe of liquid that she added to my IV.

"This is just strong Benadryl," she told me.

This seemed like an excessive amount of drama for Benadryl, but the nap I indulged in during the entire second bag of blood was a blessing. Between that and the blood itself, I felt like I could run a 5K by the time they completed the transfusion. They made me stay a little longer because I didn't have a driver, but I didn't mind. I could use this opportunity to check my emails.

As soon as I opened my phone, though, my stress level shot sky high. I had repeated text messages from Abbey.

"You're at the hospital?"

"Mom?"

"I went to your room, and they told me you left. I checked in the office, and they said you went to the hospital."

"What's going on?"

I was sure at that moment that I was the world's shittiest parent. How was it possible for me to not make sure that my children, who attended the same school where I taught, were aware that I was alright, but that I was going to receive a transfusion to increase my red blood cell count? I had an immediate sense of remorse and, to be honest, I still have lingering guilt about this one today. A simple text message could have alleviated their concern for their mom.

There are so many negative emotions connected to regret: remorse, sorrow, and helplessness. Regret increases stress along with anxiety and depression. It is not healthy. This is likely one major reason my depression spiked after I finished treatment. While undergoing treatment, my brain felt unfocused. No one who understands chemotherapy and its impact on the body would ever judge me as harshly as I judged myself. I can experience remorse for scaring my kids, but even if I could revisit that day in 2012, considering my emotional and physical state, I question my ability to have acted differently.

One of my character defects is that I tend to feel guilty even for things that aren't mine to own. Here are just a few examples. One thing my daughter has shared with me is that she hated how, without warning, her list of friends doubled. No, she didn't make more friends, but people who never used to speak to her suddenly wanted to befriend her. From my perspective, there was no intention of malice on their part. It becomes challenging when you are responsible for both your own children and the children of the entire community, who are also considered "your kids."

Those "other kids" didn't know how to deal with my cancer either. I'm sure it made them feel like they were doing something by befriending my kids. Abbey just wanted them to leave her alone.

I do feel a little bad about asking the entire staff to keep an eye on my kids. Most of them understood that I just wanted them to be there if my kids were struggling, but one staff member approached Abbey regularly in the cafeteria to talk about how she was doing. Now, if you remember anything about high school, you know that lunch is the one time when students get to socialize with their friends. This also means that if staff members are approaching you there to talk about your mom's cancer, it is embarrassing and stigmatizing to your fifteen-year-old psyche. Abbey hated it, and it still bothers her today.

In retrospect, I realize now that not everyone in that building, student or staff, was comfortable dealing with cancer. The best we can do is to use this as a learning experience. If you ever encounter someone who is diagnosed with cancer, my best advice is to offer your assistance, but also understand that the person who is sick, as well as their family members, may just need some space.

My biggest regret of all is the time and energy I spent trying to act strong for my kids. I thought I was protecting them, but like a lot of the things we do to protect our kids, it seems counterproductive to me today. Life can be challenging, and adults undergo emotional turmoil that deeply affects their innermost being. I should have allowed my kids to see that I experienced fear sometimes in order to help them in understanding that it was acceptable if they felt scared as well. Fear is simply an emotion, and at times, I perceived it as a solitary island I was stranded on. If I could have a do-over, I would have openly discussed all of that instead of attempting to make everything okay when it simply wasn't.

I have learned a lot about regret in the past decade. The main thing I've learned is that regrets need to be fact-checked. Some of my regrets are pointless. If I'm living in regret, I am holding myself to an impossible standard. Here is where I needed to practice acceptance. I have learned over the years to acknowledge that I am human, and, like all other humans, I make mistakes.

Today when I am tempted by regret, I ask three questions: Can I change it? Can I fix it? Can I learn from it? Sometimes I need to apologize, and I do that as soon as possible. That might bring about a sense of hope for the other person, but it also empowers me to progress towards forgiving myself just as I would forgive another if the situation were reversed. If I am living in regret, I am living in the past and there is very little I can do about most things that have already occurred. There is very little that is in the past that I can change and not much more that I can fix today. I can try to learn from any mistakes I made, though, and if there is a lesson to be learned, I can use that knowledge in the present. And the present is where I need to live in order to be at peace. The past holds regret, and the future holds fear, and if I spend too much time in either, I will find no serenity.

# Chapter 26

# Practicing Gratitude Can Change Your Worldview

"Gratitude is one of the strongest and most transformative states of being. It shifts your perspective from lack to abundance and allows you to focus on the good in your life, which in turn pulls more goodness into your reality."
Jen Sincero

This book arose in part from my desire to share the knowledge cancer imparted to me. One of the most significant of those realizations is that while recognizing the positive can be challenging, that doesn't mean it isn't present. As I look back at my journey, one thing I am most grateful for is the people. I experienced tremendous support, and so did my kids. The uncertainty surrounding how my kids would cope at school ranked high among my biggest fears. Throughout my life, I've seen countless teenagers collapse under the weight of hardships at home, and I was determined to shield my children from a similar outcome.

It turns out I didn't need to worry. My kids had grown up in that high school building since they were babies. I've always expressed my belief that every child should have access to at least one dependable adult in their school who they can rely on when they are facing difficulties. Hunter and Abbey had those people.

For Hunter, it was my English teacher colleague who battled breast cancer the year before I did. She could offer him reassurance in a way that perhaps no one else could. She had credibility and that made her approachable for him.

Hunter also leaned on my friend and coworker across the hall. Kam-Lin and I had coached forensics and theater together for years, and Hunter was one of Kam-Lin's theater kids. Both he and Abbey found solace in her presence, knowing they could freely share their thoughts and feelings. She was also who they went to when they needed someone to forge my signature on a permission slip. She was a solid source of support for them when I was sick.

Abbey's band director was her primary source of support. In the band room, she found so much more than her favorite teacher. My youngest child found the escape from life that she so badly needed. It was a respite from being my caretaker and from the tough realities of how things beyond her control had transformed her life. In the band room, she could be a fifteen-year-old kid again.

The other person I knew my kids could rely on in that building was my friend Lori. We met in college and had reconnected when I accepted this teaching job. She had known my kids since they were babies and they knew she was there if they needed anything. I am not sure how much they went to her, but I do know that to this day, Abbey calls Lori her BFF (best friend forever).

I don't mean to imply that these are the only people who were there for Hunter and Abbey, but these four people were pivotal in getting us through the cancer season. We can't express our gratitude enough.

Beyond the people, I cannot express enough how grateful I am for the laughter. My kids and I were able to keep our sense of humor through this journey, and that was a gift. Laughter is healing, and this would have been a much different journey without it.

There are so many examples, but this is one of my favorites. I was almost done with treatment when we went out to a Chinese buffet. I was obviously a cancer patient. I had come to terms with the fact that my hat did not conceal that information from anyone. As my two youngest kids and I were talking and finishing our meal, the server delivered our bill and three fortune cookies. I opened the plastic wrapper and snapped my cookie in half. I turned it over, looking at first one half and then the other. There was nothing there. As the sarcastic person I am, always looking for the laugh, I told the kids, "Oh my gosh, you guys, I don't have a fortune."

Not hearing the laughter coming from my teenagers and uncomfortable with what she heard, the lady at the next table stammered, "There was another lady a little while ago who didn't have one. It doesn't mean anything." She was trying so hard to be reassuring.

I covered my smile with my hand and exchanged a look with my kids. "I'm sure you're right," I responded.

We paid the bill and as soon as we walked through the door, all three of us burst into laughter. To this day, I still chuckle at the thought that she believed I would take a fortune, or lack of a fortune, at a Chinese buffet seriously. I mean, maybe if it were a sit-down restaurant, but surely not at a buffet.

Over the course of my journey through cancer, my kids grew up. I am sometimes tempted to view all of this through my regret lens, even today. They had to grow up much faster than their peers, but I still don't know what the alternative would have been. I was a single parent who faced cancer while raising teenage children. They wanted to help me, and it sucked that they were in that position, but it was what it was.

Paradoxically, today I would say my kids matured faster than their classmates. When they graduated and left for college, I never worried about their ability to take care of themselves. They had the skills required for cooking, cleaning, and taking care of themselves and others. They were familiar with the process of making appointments and doing laundry. Heck, Abbey even had a good understanding of how to ask important questions at a medical appointment.

My youngest two children knew how to study because when they were fifteen and sixteen, I did not have the energy to make sure they were doing their homework. Well, Hunter's wife (then girlfriend), Malorie, gets some of the credit for getting him to study. That's one of the reasons we jokingly refer to her as my favorite child.

My children left for college far more responsible than the average eighteen-year-old. I still wish they could have avoided experiencing what they did, but I don't regret it anymore. They are strong, self-sufficient adults and they didn't have to struggle in college like their peers did to learn basic life skills. This is what this situation looks like through my gratitude lens.

Negativity overwhelmed me when I first got sober. I could not see the positive in my life at all. Someone with longer sobriety told me I should make a gratitude list every day and it would transform my attitude. At first, it was all I could do to come up with three things to put on my list, but I did it. Then a friend told me that for every negative thought I had, I needed to come up with two positive thoughts. This is how I learned to take a negative thought and turn it around to see it through a positive lens.

During the cancer season of my life, this skill was invaluable. I held my share of pity parties, but I did not stay there. I ate something, took a nap, and looked for something positive to focus on. When I struggled to do that, I turned to paper and pen, making a good old-fashioned gratitude list. These lists have made such an impact on my life and they continue to affect me today. Whenever I am struggling with something, I make a list. There is always something to be grateful for.

# Chapter 27

# We Are Setting an Example for Others to Follow

"A good example has twice the value of good advice."
Albert Schweitzer

I f you ask a teacher about their kids, they may look at you quizzically for a moment as they try to determine "which kids" you mean. You see, teachers have their biological children and perhaps children through marriage, but they also foster a large group of children they consider their own. In the same way that I had regrets about how my cancer impacted my four children, I also grappled with how I had let down my students.

To be honest, I remember little of the 2011–2012 school year. It is all lost in the blur of brain fog I experienced as I fought cancer. I finished my chemotherapy in April, and I remember the wave of self-loathing I felt because I was sure I had failed my students. I was out of the classroom from Thanksgiving break through Christmas break; when I returned to school in January, I began chemotherapy, and I was in the classroom only seven out of every ten days for most of the remainder of the school year. Although I don't remember, I can't imagine I was an effective teacher when I was in the room. I prided myself on being a hands-on teacher, up and moving around the classroom. I did not have the energy to do that during the spring of 2012. I was exhausted by noon each day, despite the fact that I did a significant portion of my teaching from my chair.

In 2022, as I approached retirement, I thought about how tired I was after grading a batch of essays, and because I was in a pretty reflective mood, I wondered how I could possibly have graded essays the year I had cancer. I had been teaching for eighteen years when I received my cancer diagnosis and my reputation for being a tough grader preceded me. I gave tons of feedback and I made students work to become better writers. I don't remember grading a single paper that year, though. I know I did it, but I cannot imagine I could have graded essays in the same way I did every other year of my nearly three decades as a teacher. I recall the feeling of being on autopilot, just going through the motions. I shortchanged those students. I was sure they learned nothing in my class that year, and that made me sad. They would have been so much better off if they'd been in another teacher's classroom. I was struggling with imposter syndrome and feeling like I hadn't done enough, like I wasn't enough.

Springtime in high school is a busy time. One reason is that this is when all the juniors are requesting letters of recommendation from their teachers. These letters are a college application requirement and can make the difference between whether a student is accepted at the college of their choice. As an English teacher, I always received more than my fair share of requests. This year was not an exception.

The easiest letter for me to write that year was for Mike. Mike was an outstanding student. He moved here during his sophomore year from Madison, and he was not happy about it at first. This part of the state was more rural, and his friends were back in Madison. He adjusted quickly, though. He was smart, athletic, and popular. I had a wealth of examples to share in his letter. He was a talented public speaker, he was effective in class discussion, and his writing skills were excellent. One of the first things I observed about Mike when he was a sophomore was that he always seemed to be writing in a notebook and when anyone would come close, he would hide it. Later, I discovered he enjoyed creative writing. Mike was one of those kids that were just easy to teach.

It is proper etiquette for students to write a thank-you note after a teacher writes a letter of recommendation for them. Mike's thank-you note was not typical. It was almost two typed pages long. It was beautifully written, and it caught me by surprise.

Mike began by saying he knew I felt like I hadn't taught them much, but he wanted me to know that he had learned more from me than any of his other teachers that year. He said, "You taught me things that really matter. You taught me life is hard sometimes, but you still need to show up. You came to school every day with your head held high, even when I'm sure you didn't feel like it. There were mornings when I didn't feel like getting up and coming to school. Then I would think about you, and I thought if Mrs. Jeske can get out of bed and come to school when she is battling cancer, the least I can do is show up." At the end of his letter, he said, "Sometimes the most important lessons we learn are not what we expected. People teach others by example, and the example you have provided this year is one I will never forget. You showed me how to do the work even when I feel like I can't, how to fight through pain and exhaustion when I think I have nothing left to give, and how to put others before myself every single day."

I sat motionless, tears pouring from my eyes. I had just been schooled by this young man. It was at this moment that I realized kids are learning from us all the time, not only when we are actively "teaching." They are watching what we do and how we do it. They are learning what they want to do and what they don't want to do in life, who they want to be and who they don't want to be, and what they see played out by the adults around them is all part of that lesson. Wow! That is humbling, and honestly, it's a little terrifying too.

If you work with kids in any capacity, ask yourself this question: What are we really teaching them? I did not realize my mere presence at school was affecting students, and it turned out they had some idea what it was taking me every day to just walk through the door. They watched me struggle; they watched me fight, and they watched me win.

What was I teaching kids during the 2011–2012 school year? I was teaching them how to climb mountains that seem insurmountable, how to keep going when your tank is empty, and how to refuse to lie down and give up. They may not have learned as much English from me as students in other years, but they learned some important lessons—lessons I hope they are still using today to make their lives and the lives of those around them better.

# Chapter 28

---

# The Struggle Continues After the Cancer Is Gone

"Life is a long lesson in humility."
James M. Barrie

After winning my battle with cancer, I wanted to believe it was all in the past and life would return to normal again. That is not my story. My story is one of antidepressants and therapy, of time and emotional healing, of hope and continued work through my Twelve Step Program.

I expected I would experience a sense of liberation after cancer held me captive the previous year. I had my life back, but as time passed, I realized it wasn't my old life that I had back, but an entirely new one, and I wasn't sure how I felt about that.

For the first time in my life, after my cancer fight, I was genuinely afraid. I no longer possessed the false sense of security I once harbored about my life and health pre-cancer. As I channeled all my energy and determination into surviving each day's fight against cancer, nothing else had mattered. Fear gripped me in short bursts, but I had no time to indulge in it. I had kids to raise, a job to do, doctor's appointments to get to. Now I had time to breathe, and I was paralyzed by the vulnerability I felt. This was so much more significant and disabling than any anxiety I had experienced before. With therapy, this has improved over time. Still, though, I never feel safe like I did before.

I had no traces of cancer, but my health did not return to normal. Because of chemotherapy, I was now gifted with peripheral neuropathy, which left the bottoms of my feet numb. With that, I sometimes had sporadic nerve pain that shot through my feet, stopping me with a quick intake of breath where I was standing. My insurance plan included follow-up telehealth with a nurse. Every visit, she repeated how important it was to always wear shoes, even in the house. Though I wanted life to progress as though my cancer was just a bad dream, I, in all my wisdom, knew better. I hated wearing shoes in the house.

Around this time, my kids were building model brains for an anatomy class in school. This involved Styrofoam and toothpicks, among other things. I'm sure you can see where this is going. As I walked barefoot across my living room, a sharp stabbing pain in the bottom of my foot stopped me right where I stood. I hobbled over to the couch and sat down to examine it. There was a small puncture and a dot of blood, but beyond that I couldn't see what I had stepped on. I picked at the skin with a needle, and I pressed down around the puncture, but nothing materialized. Because I have no sensation in the bottom of my feet due to peripheral neuropathy, I did not feel pain until the toothpick was completely embedded in my foot. It was the oddest sensation. I couldn't feel the pressure from my fingers on my skin, but somewhere inside my foot it hurt when I applied pressure. It felt like there was something still in there, but for days I repeated this attempted extraction and nothing happened. I went to the doctor, and they did an x-ray, which obviously showed nothing, since toothpicks are made of wood and wood does not show up on an X-ray. My foot hurt, though, and I was desperate. I wasn't in pain all the time, only when I stepped just right. I absentmindedly squeezed the bottom of my foot as I watched television, but I had given up hope of ever figuring out what was going on.

Over a month passed and then one day as I was once again absentmindedly pressing on the bottom of my foot, a piece of wood shot out of my foot! Abbey said, "What was that?" as she moved to pick it up and hand it to me.

"Part of your brain," I countered as I looked at this piece of wood over an inch long. It turns out Hunter and Abbey had been breaking toothpicks in half to stick them into the Styrofoam as they built their brains. Apparently, they missed one and my foot found it. I had been carrying this inch-long piece of toothpick in my foot for over a month. I can laugh about this now, but at the time I was frustrated. Even the simplest of things, like walking across a room, would never be normal again.

My body was cancer-free, but for the first time, I realized this would not be over for a long time, if ever. I had to return to oncology in four months, and then every six months for five years. If I achieved that milestone without any cancer coming back, I would only need to visit oncology once a year. If my cancer holding me hostage for a year wasn't already terrible enough, I would also be under surveillance for at least the next ten years. That's the thing with being a cancer survivor. There is no answer to the question of whether we are cured or not. The passage of time with no new evidence of disease is the only answer we receive, and it's an awful thing to have hanging over your head for the rest of your life.

I no longer had cancer, but I was also in full-fledged menopause at forty-six. This was the first time I had been confronted with all that menopause and losing estrogen would mean in my daily life. It resulted in fatigue and sleep issues, mood swings and depression, and headaches, as well as hot flashes and night sweats. I was already dealing with insecurities and anxieties about this whole new post-cancer world I had been thrust into, only to have hormones messing with me too! How cruel and unfair! Many women seek treatment for these symptoms in the form of hormone replacement therapy (HRT), but that was not an option for me. My cancer was estrogen receptor-positive breast cancer, which meant I was not a candidate for HRT. Adding estrogen back into my body could increase the risk of the cancer returning.

For the first time in my life, my own body would not do what I asked it to do. This post-cancer version of Angela needed more rest than I ever needed before. I have had to learn to deal with almost constant feelings of muscle fatigue and weakness of varying degrees. It is like asking my car to make a full tank's journey on half a tank of gas. No matter how well rested I am, the fatigue is lurking. I have a new body with a new set of limitations, and I needed to learn to respect them. I have always given everything one hundred percent of my effort and the adjustment to being okay with anything less has been difficult. I fought this harder than maybe anything else in my cancer recovery. I fought it all the way to my retirement from teaching high school English. As I look back, I could have taken a much gentler approach and given myself a lot more grace during those ten years post-cancer.

I have learned a cancer recurrence scare can be even more terrifying than the initial cancer diagnosis because all the innocence about the brutality of fighting cancer is gone. Whenever I've had a scare, I've been painfully conscious of the world of terror that looms if cancer returns. Today, I am fortunate to have an incredible oncologist who listens attentively and promptly responds every time I fear a recurrence of cancer. She has performed brain scans when I complained about frequent headaches even though I experienced migraine headaches starting at the age of twenty-one. She never brushes me off and tells me to just wait and see. Instead, she gleefully told me my brain scan showed "no signs of any abnormalities of any kind." Two years later, when I told her I had a strange ongoing pain in my ribs, she ordered a full body bone scan. Once again, lots of arthritis throughout my body, but "no signs of abnormalities." When I have these strange aches and pains, my brain jumps to "please don't be cancer. I don't think I can do that again." It was difficult to experience this anxiety once after the initial diagnosis, but it is traumatizing to feel it for a second time, years after my cancer fight.

I have remained cancer-free for thirteen years now and I no longer require visits to my oncologist unless I have a concern. Over time and with counseling, I am able to postpone the trauma response of being sure that I have cancer and it is going to kill me this time, but it has been a long journey to get there. Today, when people ask me how I don't worry every day about my cancer returning, I tell them I refuse to spend my time that way. I may get cancer again or I may not, but I will not give cancer every day of my life until I reach that crossroads. This mindset has taken time, and it did not come without a lot of work.

After cancer, I experienced anxiety so bad that I'd find myself curled up in a fetal position in tears and not have any idea why; I found myself suffering from depression; and eventually I was diagnosed with post-traumatic stress disorder (PTSD). With help, similar to my recovery from alcoholism, I have retrained my brain to take control of my negative thoughts rather than allowing them to control me. I know I am not in control of the universe and my faith in God has been a cornerstone for me as well, and I fully believe God has brought me through this. It is a journey, not a battle, though, and journeys sometimes last a lifetime. On this journey, I have learned I can decide how I will react to the things that happen to me and to the thoughts I have about those things. Today I strive "to recognize the things I cannot change, to dig deep to find the courage to change the things I can, and to seek the wisdom to know the difference" between the two.

I now see that it wasn't as simple as going back to my pre-cancer life. Life is different and my needs as a person are different. It isn't just a new life or a new normal, but a whole new world I am living in. The anxiety and depression I experienced for months as a cancer survivor was awful, but it was also one of the best things that happened to me. It was then that I realized the need for a complete reset in my life. And that is when the real work began to figure out what I needed to do to feel whole again. I knew at long last that it was up to me to determine what my new life would look like, and I resolved to do just that.

# Epilogue: Triumph of the Human Spirit

"The best part of life is not just surviving, but thriving with
passion and compassion and humor and style and generosity
and kindness."
Maya Angelou

The other day I was talking to a friend about the COVID-19
Pandemic of 2020. I recall being told by my principal that
we would be going home in a couple of days, and we would need
to teach from there, something none of us had any idea how to
do. I remember driving through vacant cities devoid of human life.
I remember the isolation and the feeling of helplessness. When
I think about it, it's like I am watching a reel of someone else's
life. There is a level of numbness that seems almost protective. I
experienced that once more while writing this book.

On the surface, the two things seem very different. My cancer
journey and a global pandemic. Here's the thing, though, at the
conclusion of both events, I crashed. When the pandemic was
over, I thought to myself, I've done this before. Once again, I
struggled through bad days and days that weren't as bad, but I kept
putting one foot in front of the other to do what needed to be
done. At the end of the pandemic, like the end of my cancer, my
anxiety was out of control. I went back on my anxiety meds and I

put myself back in therapy. In both cases, I found myself trapped in a trauma response.

As I wrote this book, I remembered some hard days, and I remembered funny stories and laughter, but there is also a lot that I do not remember. Perhaps that is my brain shielding me, or maybe I am just growing forgetful. What I find I remember most clearly are the lessons that the cancer era of my life taught me and I have endeavored to share a few of those in these pages. These lessons have served me well in recovery, in surviving cancer, and in life.

Things are different for me today. I try to live my life with purpose. It's easy to get sidetracked, forgetting what's important, but I owe it to myself to spend my time on the things that really matter. I try to identify what my priorities are and then focus my limited energy on them. Before my cancer, I used to run around doing everything for everybody. I wanted balance in my life, but I didn't know how to get it. Today I have a clear understanding of how I want to spend my time and who I want to spend it with. I no longer need to be everything for everybody. And thank goodness for that. I will never possess the same energy I had prior to my cancer, and so I must be intentional about the choices I make.

Shortly after I finished treatment, I was doing a college visit with my son. Part of that visit was a campus tour, and as we walked around campus, I slowed down little by little. Hunter asked several times if I was okay and of course I responded each time by telling him I was fine. Then we reached these steps that take you from lower campus to upper campus. The tour guide said if there was anyone who didn't feel like they could make it up the steps, we could wait on lower campus, and they would meet us when they came back down. I wanted for Hunter to have a normal college tour experience with a normal mother and so I began the climb. Fast-forwarding a bit, we had to stop several times and by the time we returned for the last part of the tour, I knew I would not be able to do anything strenuous for the next two days. Trying to complete the entire walking tour was a mistake, and today I've realized the importance of being smarter in situations like that.

In some perverse way, cancer has improved my life. I still focus on having a positive attitude, and I try to see the beauty around me. Admittedly, this is sometimes difficult in a world filled with so much that is negative, but cancer taught me how powerful a positive attitude and a sense of humor can be. I will never forget my banter with my chemo nurses, and while some of it was acting "as if" until I believed what I was selling, it still made me feel better. If it worked when I had cancer, why wouldn't it work now? Life still happens and I still struggle sometimes, but today I see problems as an opportunity to learn and grow. When I start to travel down the road of negativity, it's time to look in the mirror and initiate a serious heart-to-heart with myself.

There are so many people who helped me when I was struggling. I had amazing doctors, and I can't even begin to say enough about my nurses. The oncology and chemotherapy nurses are the glue that holds everything together. They are some of the most empathetic individuals I have ever encountered. They tell stories and they listen to yours. They laugh with you and they hold your hand (or bring you a heated blanket) when you are sad. They can ask about your diarrhea and your new puppy in the same breath, and it doesn't even surprise you when they do. Those nurses and my friends and family gave me grace when I struggled, and I strive to do the same for others today. I don't always do that perfectly, but my journey is about "progress, not perfection."

Perhaps the hardest thing of all has been to learn to love myself unconditionally. I have struggled so much with self-loathing during my lifetime and especially during this journey. I felt unattractive and undesirable almost every day when I had cancer, and that didn't automatically change when a doctor said, "You are cancer-free." My appearance has been forever altered by cancer. It has been a journey to learn the importance of self-love and acceptance and that has been a key to my healing from within and addressing my anxiety and depression issues.

I experience intense emotions even today, and I acknowledge and accept them. I let myself sit in my room and cry and I let myself laugh hysterically. I have learned that if I just walk through my feelings, they don't last nearly as long, and then I can get on with my life.

I don't accept people in my life who hurt me because life is too short for that. I used to believe I wasn't worthy of love and respect, but that is not true. I have come to the realization that I can be my authentic self, without the need to apologize to anyone for being who and what I am.

Finally, I celebrate every single birthday wholeheartedly and without reservation. I just turned sixty and you better believe I celebrated that big number. I get to be sixty! Not everyone is so lucky.

Nobody wants to hear a doctor say, "You have cancer," but it isn't always a death sentence either. Sometimes it is an opportunity. In my lifetime, I have learned that sometimes we need to go through hard times to grow and learn. My life will never be the same after my experience with this disease, and to tell the truth, I don't want it to be. The fears I faced, the gratitude I learned, and the growth I experienced are something I never want to forget.

Cancer is a part of my journey and without it, I would not be the person I am today. I am married to a wonderful man who loves me with all my flaws. I am the parent of seven children (including my stepchildren), and I have been fortunate to be gifted with eleven beautiful grandchildren. I am incredibly lucky to have all that I do and to navigate it all with the knowledge I have gained along the way. I wouldn't change a thing. My cancer was a chapter in my life, not the whole story. There is no going back and I am not in control of what lies ahead. All I can do is stay in the moment, be gentle with myself and others, and live with gratitude for all that cancer taught me.

# Acknowledgements

This book was in my head in one form or another for over a decade. I needed time and distance before I was ready to write it. I also needed for the noise in my head to quiet a bit to make room for the process of getting the story onto paper. Retiring from a teaching career and trying to figure out who I was now and what my next steps might be provided the gentle nudge I needed.

My friend Kim and I used to talk about starting a writing group, but as long as we were still teaching it was just a pipe dream. After we retired, she actually started the group. That group has been pivotal in this book becoming a reality. I want to thank Kim Butnick, Dana Parisi, and Jamie Wolf for being my sounding board at the beginning when all I knew was that I wanted to write about my cancer journey. I also want to thank them for supporting my dream when I posed this crazy idea of combining a story about recovery from cancer with a story about recovery from alcoholism. I want to acknowledge the other members of the writing group who have joined us along the way. I am grateful for your feedback and your patience. Thanks for believing in me before I believed in myself.

I also want to thank my recovery communities in both La Crosse and Eau Claire, Wisconsin. I am not sure where I would be without you, especially the women who supported me when things were looking bleak. I love you all and am so proud to have "trudged the road of happy destiny" with each and every one of you. Thanks for the lessons.

I would be remiss if I didn't acknowledge all of the medical professionals who go to work every day and make life just a bit easier for countless cancer patients. I especially want to hold up my chemotherapy nurses. Your job is one of the most difficult I can imagine, but the empathy with which you meet that task is unparalleled.

To the staff I was blessed to work with at Holmen High School, I will love you forever. Thank you for being there for me and my kids. I'm not sure how we would have made it through this journey without your support.

This book would not be the book it is without my beta readers Jeff McLain, Carrie Carlson, Jen Kronenberg, and Roxie Drung and my editor Bess Maher. I am also grateful to the designers at Miblart Services for designing my beautiful cover.

Finally, I want to thank my family for their support of this memoir because this isn't just my story; it is also theirs. I want to give a special shout-out to my daughter, Abbey. Not everyone has what it takes to be their mom's cancer caregiver at the age of 15. I am forever grateful that you were willing and able to do far more than I ever wanted to ask of you.

www.ingramcontent.com/pod-product-compliance
Lightning Source LLC
Chambersburg PA
CBHW021152130626
46554CB00005B/1775